D1413440

BEYOND 2000 . . .

... Medical advances extend human life by decades.

... AIDS spreads out of control in Africa

... Cosmic chaos threatens the end of civilization

... Cyclones, earthquakes, floods, and volcanos kill millions

... Great War between China and India kills 28 million and is ended with US superweapon

... Nuclear power plants worldwide are shut down after disaster in Florida

... Kevorkian camps are opened worldwide

... Computer-vaccine systems keep the world healthy

... Evangelical ministers dominate electronic highway

... Roman Catholics split over election of black pope

... The first colony on Mars is declared a permanent settlement

... Crime disappears from the streets of America

SHAWN ROBBINS'
PROPHECIES FOR THE END OF TIME

SHAWN ROBBINS
and
EDWARD SUSMAN

AVON BOOKS ◆ NEW YORK

SHAWN ROBBINS' PROPHECIES FOR THE END OF TIME is
an original publication of Avon Books. This work has never before
appeared in book form.

AVON BOOKS
A division of
The Hearst Corporation
1350 Avenue of the Americas
New York, New York 10019

Copyright © 1995 by Shawn Robbins and Edward Susman
Cover photo by J.K. Potter
Published by arrangement with the authors
Library of Congress Catalog Card Number: 94-94472
ISBN: 0-380-77694-4

First Avon Books Printing: January 1995

AVON TRADEMARK REG. U.S. PAT. OFF. AND IN OTHER COUNTRIES, MARCA
REGISTRADA, HECHO EN U.S.A.

Printed in the U.S.A.

RA   10 9 8 7 6 5 4 3 2 1

Table of Contents

1	Journey into the Unknown	1
2	Africa	16
3	America, the Expansionist	29
4	The Guide	39
5	New Jobs/Technology	48
6	Home Seekers	65
7	Health Issues	75
8	Mall Incident	81
9	The Middle East	88
10	Asteroids	102
11	Asteroids 2	112
12	Kevorkian Camps	121
13	Quakes, Floods, and Fires	133
14	Ukraine Axis	143
15	South Africa	153
16	Religion in the 21st Century	162
17	A New Hawaii	173
18	Mission to the Stars	182

19	Baseball	192
20	Crime Prediction	200
21	Conclusion	206
22	Chronology	213

1

Journey Into the Unknown

I SHIVERED IN THE CAR AS WE SPED EAST ON THE New York Thruway during an unseasonably cool July morning.

Suddenly I felt an invisible tug at the back of my neck. It startled me, but it didn't frighten me. When you are psychic, however, you never ignore these things.

"We have to stop," I told my business partner, who was busily trying to set a land speed record between Syracuse and New York City.

"Stop? What do you mean, 'stop'? Where?" she said.

I looked up just as we passed the Shrine of Our Lady of Martyrs in Auriesville, N.Y.

"We have to go here," I said, pointing to the huge expanse of grassy hillside that marked the shrine.

She looked at me strangely. She knows that I am psychic and she also knows that I'm not a churchgoer— that I am, at best, agnostic. "We have to go here," I repeated.

A few miles down the road, the next exit, Fultonville, appeared. We exited the Thruway, paid our toll, and asked directions to the shrine. The shrine was four miles from the exit, and the way was well marked.

A calmness enveloped me and I felt a gnawing fear climbing my spine. I could feel the hair on the back of my neck begin to tingle.

We arrived at the shrine about 10:15. The air was heavy with a mist; the sky was overcast; the temperature was in the low fifties.

I walked around the green lawns of the immaculately maintained shrine. Near one wooden building, I was struck by the plain alabaster white statue of a Native American maiden. The woman was holding a cross against her chest and she seemed to be staring at me. A post revealed that the statue was that of Kateri Tekakwitha, "born in this Indian village Ossernenon 1656."

I paused in front of the statue and gazed into the stone eyes. Something inside me shuddered as I looked into those eyes—eyes that somehow seemed to stare back at me as if there was thought behind them in that eerily white stone.

The path around the statue led to a huge circular church. I found myself walking towards it. But with every other step, I turned back to see if those mysterious eyes of Kateri Tekakwitha were following me. I wasn't afraid but I had the uncanny feeling that I was being watched and evaluated.

I took one last look at the statue. I could feel the eyes of the Indian woman pierce my back, but strangely I didn't feel threatened. If anything the feeling was one of comfort. I opened the huge wooden door of the church and walked inside. The church was empty. I remember thinking, How many years has it been since I last walked into a church?

I sat in one of the pews at the back of the church, and waited—but I had no idea for what I was waiting.

A ray of sun escaped from behind the clouds and swept into the church, illuminating the pulpit. Instantly a wave of blue light pulsed from the pulpit, filled the church, and washed over me; immediately a similar wave of red appeared and traveled the same course; then a brilliant golden-yellow light rolled through the structure.

I became aware of a sound that wasn't a sound—a sound that echoed in my ears but wasn't a sound. The sound was clear. It was a message: "The final warning to the world."

And then it was over.

I trembled in the pew trying to regain my composure. My heart was pounding rapidly. Each beat sounded like a thunderous explosion in my ears. I tried to get up but a wave of nausea overcame me. "Oh, God," I cried, "what is happening to me?" Suddenly a wave of cold air rushed over me, and the blood in my veins turned ice cold. I had a foreboding feeling the worst was yet to come.

My business partner met me outside the church. "Are you all right?" she asked. "Sure," I lied. "How about some lunch?" she asked.

"Lunch? What time is it?"

"It's one o'clock."

I glanced at my watch. It had stopped at exactly 10:15 AM, the moment I entered the church. I had been in the trance almost three hours. It seemed like minutes to me.

In the distance the sound of thunder echoed in the air. Lightning flashed across the sky. I sensed it was a message for me to return home immediately.

We got in the car just as the rain started. The ride home was long and monotonous. The rhythmic sound of the rain hitting the car's windshield lulled me into a state of semi-sleep. I had a vivid flashback to 1974 when I dreamed about a terrifying event in the future. It began with a fog.

Slowly the fog began to clear. I was asleep. I was dreaming. I knew I was having a psychic dream. All my dreams which meant something about the future started with the fog. But this dream somehow seemed more real than any others I'd had until now.

The fog lifted, and then cleared. I can remember tensing in my sleep, knowing that something important was going to occur. Pay attention, Shawn, I dreamed to myself. Details—names, dates, places, colors, pain, joy, happiness, betrayal—became clearer, focused, intense.

Don't be afraid, I told myself, you know what is happening. Let it happen.

I was in an airplane. It was immense. There were nine people across each of the aisles. I couldn't see the entire plane. I was sitting in one cabin of this plane and I could hear conversations taking place. There were people talking in English, which, of course, I understood easily. But there were other languages spoken as well—French I recognized—even though I don't speak the language well. A guttural tongue washed through my dream. It sounded Middle Eastern. I wasn't familiar with it.

I was fascinated by the size of the aircraft. It was 1974. The age of the jumbo jet had just begun. Airbuses that dwarfed the small 150-passenger planes were being flown all over the globe—and not just by the major carriers. Every nation that flew had to have its own jumbo jet. The 747s, L-1011s, and DC-10s were finding their way to every airport in the world.

My psychic dreams are strange in that even though I'm aware that I'm dreaming, there is another feeling of being part of the dream, part of the event, a piece of the future.

I looked around me at scores of people—men, women, children. I knew I was in an airplane, yet it was unfamiliar. I could not see where the cockpit was. I could not see where the tail was. It seemed as if I was in a gigantic living room or movie theater. It felt like a plane, though. We were climbing. I could feel the air pressure in my ears as we rose. I was pressed back into my seat as the plane climbed higher into the sky.

I knew the names of some of the passengers and saw their recent memories. I remember seeing the Eiffel Tower and realizing that the plane was taking off from

Paris. The memories were of a vacation. People were going home. The mood was happy and cheerful.

I remember thinking to myself as I dreamt, "I feel so wonderful. Why am I so terrified?"

The impact of the floor of the plane collapsing reached me as a feeling rather than as a sound. I saw faces of joy turn instantly skeletal. There were calls of surprise, quickly followed by shrieks of horror—cries that filled my head even as they were swallowed by a hurricane of wind and debris of papers, books and bits of luggage. The refuse swirled in the air and whipped towards the rear of the aircraft. I watched as my fellow passengers groped for falling oxygen masks as the plane decompressed. I shuddered even as I slept as I watched one after another person go blue from lack of oxygen, pass out from fear, and from the terror of facing certain painful, mutilating death.

I thrashed in bed and heard the unbearable panicked screams that blended in with the horrifying whine of the now rapidly descending airplane. My psychic dreambody removed my body from the passenger in which it was residing. I was floating above the passenger and then outside the airplane, riding along as if I were some helpless guide to the Netherworld.

Faster and faster the great aircraft plunged. I could see that the plane had three engines, curiously one of them actually went right through the tail of the aircraft. The design fascinated me. I'd never seen something like that before. That wasn't that surprising because I didn't travel by plane that often and I wasn't interested in aircraft design. I could see a large hole along the right side of the plane, below the passenger deck of the airplane.

I watched transfixed as the disaster unfolded before my closed eyes as I lay in my bed. I saw the plane plummet toward the woods below. Nothing seemed to be slowing its flight. With unrelenting speed it pressed toward its own doom. Closer and closer to death it fell, its engines screaming out of control.

As it neared the treetops, the plane remarkably began to level off. For an instant I was confused—my psychic powers told me that no one was going to survive, that no one could control this plane, that disaster was only seconds away. Yet it seemed that at the very last second, a miracle had occurred; that somehow the brave pilots had regained control of the aircraft. It gave me a psychic moment to observe the plane. I couldn't read the name of the airline, the lettering was readable, but it didn't make sense to me at the time. I could see enough to know that it was an international carrier— not a US plane or any of the major international companies I was familiar with such as BOAC or Air France or KLM.

Then came the moment I will never forget and hope to God that I never have to recall. The plane struck the trees. It struck with such incredible force that it sheared off the tops of the trees as if it were some giant scythe. I could feel the pain of death as it seared instantly through the passengers as the plane disintegrated in flames—its majestic metal frame torn to ribbons.

The awful pain raced through me as the souls of 346 people passed in an instant. I saw a tombstone that read "March 3, 1974." I saw a watch tossed into the air, floating in an ethereal breeze, its shattered face reading "12:40."

I awoke, sweating, nauseous, a taste of blood, smoke, and oil in my mouth. I knew what I had seen. I reached for a piece of paper and began writing down what I had seen. The first thing I wrote was, "3/3/74, 12:40 PM." I knew it happened in the daytime because I could see daylight.

I then remembered to look at my calendar. It was February 16, 1974. I wrote down everything I could recall about my dream. I wrote down names of people I remembered in the dream. I wrote down the description of the aircraft. I kept writing until daylight appeared through my apartment window in New York City.

I threw on some clothes; put on my shoes and coat. I raced down to the corner newsstand. I thought, "Was it a psychic dream of something happening in the future? Did I dream something and receive telepathic communication of a simultaneous event? Was it a dream of an event in the past?" I had to know. I bought every paper at the stand. There was nothing in any of them about any aircraft accident.

I called up one of my friends on the *New York Post* and asked him to look for any stories about airplane crashes anywhere in the world. He found nothing from the wire services. Then he transferred me to the newspaper morgue, but no one could find any story about a jumbo jet crashing.

I shook and shook. I knew that this unprecedented disaster was going to take place. I knew the time. I knew the place. I knew the date.

But I didn't know how to stop it.

Finally I decided to call the Federal Bureau of Investigation. Some poor soul there took my call and listened politely, even asking questions as if he really believed what I was saying. I think he thought he was just being kind to some demented individual. I could understand perfectly what his problem would be: Do I stop every plane from flying out of Paris on March 3 because some woman claims it's going to fall out of the sky?

At that point I realized what a gift and what a curse psychic powers could be. I could see the future, I could predict disaster—and yet there wasn't anything I could do to prevent it from happening. No one was going to treat me as a prophet and believe my predictions of disaster; no one was going to repent their sins because Shawn Robbins said their plane was going to go down in flames. No matter how right I was, no one would believe me until it was too late—and then they would say: "What an unbelievable coincidence!"

And I knew that these nay-sayers were correct. The proof of my prediction would only be believed after it was true—and by then 346 people would be dead in the forests outside of Paris.

The FBI man took down all my information and said he'd look into what I'd said. But even as he said it I knew that those poor people were doomed.

Every day as March 3 approached, I waited with dread. Maybe I was wrong? Lord knows I hoped I was wrong. Maybe something would intervene. I remembered the fog of my dream. Maybe, I hoped, it would be too foggy to take off on March 3? I went over to the New York City library and began looking at pictures of new airplanes. I opened one book and my heart froze. There was the plane in my dream. One huge engine under each wing and one engine that looked as if it had been shot through the middle of the high-standing tail. Under the picture was a caption. This was a DC-10.

I was eating breakfast on March 3, figuring that I would be too nervous to eat lunch because that was the time I saw for the accident. The radio was playing music as I tried to keep my mind off the plane by doing the *New York Times* crossword puzzle. The 9 AM news came on, with a lead story that a Turkish Airlines plane had crashed near Paris. Details, the announcer said, were sketchy.

For a moment I didn't react. The plane I saw crashing wouldn't crash until after noon. And anyway, how could Turkish Airlines own a huge plane like a DC-10. It took a few seconds for my rattled mind to understand. In Paris, it was already past noon. The guttural language I heard in my dream-trance state was Turkish; the writing on the plane in my dream came into focus—Turkish Airlines.

Subsequent newscasts confirmed by worst fears. Everything I had seen in my psychic dream had come true.

Deep in my stomach, I felt a growl of pain: Will anyone ever believe me when I have a warning? What good are psychic powers to see the future if no one will listen? Why should I even try to reveal these visions if no one will heed them? I went through a terrible period of despair and depression. I thought that I should have been able to have prevented what occurred thousands of miles away. For months—even after it was revealed that I had correctly predicted the disaster—I forced myself to awaken if I was having a dream that seemed psychic in nature.

I told myself, There is no sense in knowing if there is nothing you can do about it.

It was in mid-summer of 1974. The events of the previous March still shrouded my psyche like a damp blanket. I lost weight, I was morose, I was awful to be around or to be associated with. I was suddenly famous, but it didn't help.

Then one muggy, hot, and noisy New York night, I dreamt again. This time I found myself pillared in the colonial stocks, watching helplessly as the citizenry dressed in modern clothes marched by, shaking their heads disapprovingly. A voice—was it God? Was it some other ultimate power?—resounded around me. None of the populace of the great city appeared to hear the booming tones.

The voice admonished me: "What right do you have to reject My gift? You've been selected to give these messages to My people. You have no right to reject these messages. To reject My messages is to reject Me and you cannot do this. Do you understand?"

I cried out in my dream, "But no one will listen. Why are You torturing me by giving me a message that will be ignored by the people You want to help?"

The voice pounded back, filling my body with fear, sending a tingling from the nape of my neck to my toenails.

"How dare you," the voice thundered, "have the temerity to believe that You could understand My purpose in giving you this gift. All you have to know is that you have My gift and you are to use My gift as best you can. I know why you have been given My gift. That's all you have to know. All you have to do is share My gift with the world. That's all you need to know. That's all that is necessary for you to know."

Suddenly, my hands and legs were free. My colonial garb vanished and I was wearing up-to-date clothing and walking the street. I felt good. I felt strong. I felt happy. I smiled at people on the street. They ignored me. I laughed out loud and they walked on by barely giving me a glance. In New York City people laughed and cried without reason all the time, and no one took heed.

But now I knew what I had to do. I had to tell the world about my dreams, my visions, my interpretations of the future. And if I do that then perhaps someone may listen. Someone may not get on a certain flight; a politician may change his vote—another may not change his; someone will not go to a certain train station or meet a certain friend from college or vote for a new school bond.

I don't know if what I say will make an iota of difference to the way things happen. I just know that this is what I must do. This is what I was chosen to do by Whomever or Whatever does the choosing in this universe.

This is what I see.

The sound of screeching brakes awoke me from my semisleep. I looked up to see the car in front of us skidding out of control on the wet roadway. A surge of adrenaline shot through my body. I closed my eyes and braced myself for what I thought would be imminent death. I saw the same lights I had seen earlier in the church, pulsating in the darkness. Suddenly I knew we would be protected from the danger in front of us. The spinning car slid by us, bumped a concrete storm-drainage manhole, and stopped its skid. Traffic eased around the vehicle as the driver warily managed to move the car forward.

We arrived back in New York about 8 PM. My business partner dropped me off in front of my home in Greenwich Village. When I opened the front door I felt a strange presence in the apartment. I knew I wasn't alone. Whoever or whatever it was was trying to communicate with me.

The visions began almost as soon as I sat at my desk. It was a repeat of the trancelike state I found myself in at the shrine. Now the images appeared at a slower pace.

It was as if I had recorded them on my VCR at "fast forward" speed and now I was reviewing the images in slow motion. There seemed to be no particular order to the way the images flowed. Sometimes I'd see one vision and it would change into a second and different image and then would revert to its original message.

Intuitively, I knew that I should just keep writing as each prophetic vision flashed to the surface. Later I could review what I was writing and interpret that which wasn't obvious. Now it was just important to put the thoughts which were hurtling through space, time, and mind on paper.

The fog that is always a part of my psychic dreams and omens parted abruptly and a wave of color appeared and in the color I could see names, faces, machinery, explosions, maps. "These are keys to the future," I thought as I wrote, my mind and body divided into separate functioning compartments. I was seeing the image with one part of my mind, but just like a split-screen television, I was thinking about what I was seeing with a different part of my brain. A third part of my body was writing the thoughts and the visions. And all this was happening in a trance. I marvel at the ability to do these things simultaneously, realizing even as I am doing them that if I weren't in the trance, I couldn't do anything.

There were faces coming towards me, angry faces. There was the man with the large neck and dark hair. His body was wide, and he pounded his hands with force on a podium. He was surrounded by a red aura, not the aura of love but an aura of flame. Instinctively, I recognized a violent man, capable of leading violent people. The redness of the scene could only mean one thing—war, conflict.

Here was an individual who held the power to thrust the world into deadly conflict. I struggled to find his identity, but nothing helped. His language was strange-sounding to me. I cursed my refusal in school to dedicate myself to language. His voice was harsh, but I couldn't immediately identify which language he was speaking.

The scene began to dissolve. Frantically I pleaded with the Force or Power that was sending these images to me. "Help me. Give me some answers." I berated myself for taking so little interest in the world. I knew I was looking at a key to the future and yet I didn't know what it was that I was seeing.

As the man's features began to dissolve something distinct began to take shape. His nose became printed words, his mouth became wiry with little squiggles, his cheeks and ears changed from one color to another, merged, and then stood apart. And then there was a map where the man's head had been. I recognized some cities. Kiev—the capital of the Ukraine—was there, and superimposed over the city, suspended above it was the tangible feeling of fear—a fear that emanated from the city outward across the countryside, across the borders into Russia on the east and Poland to the west.

To the north and south, the fear gave way to pride. The nation of Belarus, the Baltics were clearly defined. But to the south, a reddish-brown ooze—"Oh God, that's blood!" I realized—covered the area near Romania. I looked to the east and saw the giant country of Russia and I saw confusion. Fear and confusion reigned across the giant nation.

The map blurred and bent out of focus, replaced by a scene in a great hall. Men and women were waving papers and fists at each other; men on a podium vainly tried to keep order; the tricolored flag of Russia flowed without moving behind the scene. There was obvious argument, discussion, worries, fears, plans. At once, I recognized what was happening. The forces of democracy had taken hold in Russia, but elsewhere the scene wasn't as promising.

The Ukraine and White Russia (Belarus) and the Baltics had formed some unified arrangement. Was I looking at another Axis? I shuddered. Was Russia too weak a democracy to defend itself against a unified totalitarian force? What had become of the people of Moldova and Romania where the map had been smeared in blood?

I knew the answers were there, somewhere. The Power that was giving me these images would surely assist me in defining what these images meant. I was confident of this and in fact, that is exactly what would happen. But there was no time to put the puzzle together because the face of the image was changing again.

This time I saw the face of a child being carried into a hospital. The boy was just about four or five years old and tears and terror showed on his face. His parents were with him. They seemed to be sophisticated, almost aristocratic in bearing. They too emitted visions of fear and concern. Disease hovered over them, but I could see a blue aura surrounding the child and a yellow light inside his torso. I knew that this child was sick, but that whatever treatment he was getting would be successful.

The blue aura covered his head and was of such strength of color, I knew that he would defeat whatever was hurting him at this time. I saw a disease being thrown off by the body. The child will live, I said to myself, and then I began to wonder why I was being shown this image. Many children get sick and then get better. Why is this child special? I asked myself as the image faded. Is he going to be a world leader? Is this the scientist who will find an answer to the plagues of the world? I didn't know. I couldn't guess. But I knew he was important and that my answer would come in some form or another.

Even as I tried to see clues in the fading psychic tapestry, another form burst forth. This time I knew what the image was: The distinct mushroom cloud shape brought tears to my eyes. The future will suffer from nuclear holocaust, I knew. When? Where? How? The cloud disappeared and the map of India began to emerge from the ashes of fallout. Flames consumed the paper map, revealing the charred and blistered bodies of teeming millions. I could smell the burning flesh. I nearly gagged over the odor of death that flowed with the awful image.

Nuclear war in India? I asked myself. Is that possible? How could such a thing happen? And who was fighting whom? Another mystery. Another scene emerged from the chaos and grit of destruction.

The scene began in a field of orange and slowly emerged to a chaotic scene of celebration. People were smiling and dancing in the streets. Vehicle traffic had stopped and people were embracing. I recognized the Western Wall of the Temple in Jerusalem, considered one of the holiest sites in Judaism and I saw the great Dome of the Rock and realized I was looking at a celebration in Jerusalem.

I could scarcely breathe. Was I seeing an end to the centuries of conflict between Jews and Arabs over Israel? Yes, yes. Those were Arabs embracing religious Jews who were wearing traditional yarmulkes or skull caps; also prominent in the scene was a red-robed black man wearing the vestments of the pope. Somehow the future showed that peace would come to the Holy Land. Would the Power that was showing this future to me reveal how it happened? The scene slowly faded with another burst of color, but my final feeling as the velvet purple shade overtook the scene was a feeling of sadness. How could something so joyful be so sad, I wondered.

For hour upon hour these visions moved in and out of focus. Through this implosion of mind and soul I was reviewing myriad events that were yet to occur. Somehow in all this information was the key to the future. Amid the wreckage of aircraft and the buildings towering miles into the sky, mixed up with violent volcanoes and remarkable medical advances, were the answers.

I knew from the past that the Power sending me these ideas would help me discover the answers. I wrote down everything—no matter how ridiculous it seemed (was the "Cleveland Lakers" winning the World Series three times in a row important?)—because there had to be a reason for the Power to give me that information.

The only time I took a break from writing was when I could no longer keep my eyes open or when my stomach demanded food. I filled four pads with notes. I wrote more than two hundred pages in these books; I suffered from what I thought would be terminal writer's cramp; and I thought I would sleep for a week after I finished, when the visions no longer rolled through my mind.

I thought the toughest part of the chore was over. I was wrong. It was only just the beginning.

2

AFRICA

IT WAS PAST MIDNIGHT—A DARK AND STORMY NIGHT. The urgency of the phone ringing this late at night frightened me. I wondered who could be calling me at such a late hour. Nervously, I picked up the receiver and heard a voice on the other end exclaim, "I can't believe it! You did it again!"

I recognized the deep baritone of Steve Cannon, the radio talk-show host in Columbus, Ohio. Over the years Steve and I have become good friends. He's asked me to be on his show many times, and it's always been fun to talk with him and his audience. I recognized the voice but I didn't know what he was talking about.

"Hi, Steve. How are you, and what in the world are you talking about?"

"Somalia, Shawn, Somalia. Just like you predicted on the last show. You said, 'The world will be shocked into action to help children dying by the hundreds in Africa.' And look what has happened. World opinion forced the UN to go to Somalia to save the people."

I had made that prediction on his show just a few weeks before the United Nations (mainly using United States troops) made the decision to try and save the

people of Somalia. I had been predicting famine and
hunger and starvation in Africa for several years. Now,
I'm not shy about taking credit for my own predictions
that come true, but I've come to realize that it's other
people who determine if you are psychic. Obviously, if
the world were to allow psychics to decide if they are
right or not every psychic would find a way to claim
every interesting event in the world.

I told Steve that maybe my prediction was a bit too
vague to be considered a psychic hit. "Nonsense," he
said. "The way you described those children, the haunted
looks of their mothers and the dreadful stories of fathers
watching their children die one by one. It's almost as if
you were holding up a mirror to the future."

Steve went on: "Everytime I see another story on
CNN or the networks, all I can think is, 'My God,
that's just what Shawn Robbins said the last time she
was on the show.'

"And that's not all, Shawn, dozens of my listeners
called up to remind me that you had predicted Somalia.
It's not just me that thinks you were right; it's my audience, too. I might be wrong, but they are not; they are
true skeptics. The people in Columbus don't go run in
the streets every time a psychic predicts the world will
end. They know what's true and what isn't. And they're
the ones that confirmed what I was thinking. You hit it
again."

When it was announced that troops were going to
Somalia, I was relieved because I had seen the suffering there and in other parts of the continent, but I was
troubled as well because I knew that the dispatching of
United Nations troops to Somalia meant that my visions
at Auriesville were going to come true as well.

There are times when my predictions are so vivid
and detailed—the Turkish DC-10 crash for one—that
no interpretation is necessary. All the facts are there
in a straightforward, easily digested manner. All I have
to do is just repeat what I saw in the vision. But these

psychic visions are rare—terrifying and wonderful at the same time, but rare.

Other visions require interpretation. They are puzzles, full of clues and hints and words and pictures that come at me from all angles; some are pertinent to the subject, and others are just red herrings. The visions at Auriesville came as if I was watching television and getting fifty stations on one channel: One "broadcast" would come through clearly and then would abruptly fade to another "program" that would be full of static and then that would fade to a split screen "program" with two unrelated messages being played opposite each other; sometimes the "screen" I was viewing held multiple images, often overlapping each other.

Does this mean one vision is more important than another? Does one vision relate to the other? These are the questions I have to answer. From my work in the past I realize that all the answers are there, somehow hidden in the mental jigsaw puzzle. All I have to do is rearrange thousands of pieces of the puzzle until the picture focuses.

My vision of Africa, a dark and awful picture, was full of fading pictures. Scenes moved in and out of focus; colors, which I knew from my experiments with the CIA in 1971 were meaningful, shaded the scene but failed to give me identifiable clues; bits and pieces of events, people, maps, and colors filtered through the vision. I wrote it all down because I could never be sure if just a minor detail would prove to be a major inkling of the future.

There has been suffering in Africa for generations. We have all been appalled at the lines of the starving, the faces of human skeletons waiting in the desert for a few scraps of rice or a thimbleful of water. Those faces were specters in my vision, changing by staying the same. They were ghosts of the future. The pictures I was seeing were disturbing and sorrowful, and puzzling.

Especially mysterious was the one bright face I saw that seemed to cover almost every event I saw—whether that event pertained to Africa or something else. The face was childlike, but it wasn't a child; the face had distinct outlines and features—I'm sure I'll recognize it anywhere—but the race of the person was not discernible. Even the sex was impossible to detect—at first I was sure that the face was that of a young man, but the more it appeared the more it seemed to have the softness of a woman's features. I knew that this face—this person—was important, almost critical to the future, to someone's future, to the world's future. But the clues I received weren't clues to his/her identity. The clues that surrounded the image of the face, however, led me to a portrait of the future.

My vision of the faces of the Africans became strong. All the people were emaciated, with huge eyes that stared through to my soul. They pleaded for help in silence, knowing that they were doomed, yet the fire in their eyes blazed with the desire for more than just a hopeless death. I wondered how I could help them as they flashed before me.

When I had the opportunity, I sat down and reviewed the writings that I made after the visit to Auriesville. I tried to separate information from one topic to another. It was generally easy to understand when I was dealing with the peoples of Africa. There were dark faces with grieved expressions, wearing the dress of the desert or the jungle or the bright garments of the priests and leaders of proud and ancient tribes. The colors of the fabric were greens and browns and reds of earth, grasses, and the blood of animals. There was the yellow representing crops and black showing the darkness of the homelands and the countryside at night where the only light was the pinpoints of stars in the ebony sky.

Through all these scenes was an overlay of light blue. Even in the darkest scenes, I could see this blue tint— a blue with hints of white lines through it. The sky, I thought at first. But all my visions of the sky show the sky as it is: filled with clouds, with grays portending storms and the oranges of sunrise and sunset. Rarely do we see sky so blue and so constantly blue. I realized that blue was a symbol. Could blue mean a flag? I asked myself. The only flag I knew of that shade was the flag of Israel. Israel in Africa? I thought. It didn't make sense.

Not that logic has much to do with psychic ability or psychic predictions. Most people have some psychic sense, but since psychic ability has nothing to do with what we learn in school, people disregard their psychic gifts. Some people actually strive to overcome their own psychic tendencies by denying and ignoring the warnings they receive.

When children display psychic ability many parents will try to play down the gift, even punish the child for creating a scene by claiming an ability to predict; or worse a child will make a prediction—perhaps of a death in the family—and when it comes true, the parent or elder will blame the child and claim that the event was willed by the child. Still there are open-minded individuals who accept that psychic phenomena is possible, can be corralled and can be put to use—either to benefit mankind or to perform evil deeds.

In 1971, the Central Intelligence Agency in Washington became aware that in the Soviet Union work was underway with psychics to determine if psychics could be used for military purposes. The CIA began conducting its own experiments as well. I was selected among several other psychics to undergo studies.

A series of experiments proved that my brain worked differently than other peoples' brains, even differently than other psychics'. One experiment involved setting up flashing strobe lights in an enclosed, darkened room to determine if that had an effect on brain waves. The studies showed that on me strobe lights triggered brain wave patterns that are linked to psychic abilities. I was psychically sensitive to the lights, the researchers told me.

So today, twenty years later, I've found that when I need to enhance my natural psychic powers, I can do it by setting up my own strobe light system to help me with a vision. I've become so sensitized to the strobe light phenomenon that just a single flash will trigger a vision.

In November of 1992, I was walking along First Avenue in Manhattan. A friend was in town for a United Nations conference. He asked me to meet him at the UNESCO gift shop at the UN building. As I approached the visitors entrance, a group of Japanese tourists began taking snapshots of the UN building, their friends, and themselves. I smiled as I watched a New Yorker's stereotype: The Asian with a camera. About twenty various cameras suddenly fired their strobe flashes.

Instantly I was in a trance. I was looking at the blue-tinged faces of Africa again. Faces covered with fear, foreboding, and grief; other faces with tears of heartache, yet brimming with hope. In that twinkling of lights in the afternoon the meaning of my African vision came shining through—it was a vision of unparalleled sadness, unspeakable disaster, death and hopelessness for millions upon millions of people. The most frightful part of the vision to me was that I knew that the future I was seeing now was part of my future: I am going to live to see these visions of Africa come to pass in the early twenty-first century—from about the turn of the century to 2014.

Somalia, I saw in my visions, is just the beginning of United Nations' involvement in Africa. UN troops will remain in Somalia for years, attempting to disarm the roaming bands of thugs who have caused so much turmoil, hardship, death, and starvation. While the imminent death of tens of thousands of Somalis will be averted by the UN presence, the sky-blue flag with its white design will continue to fly over Somalia for decades. The reason, of course, is that the UN will find no one who is willing to govern the land or who will be accepted as governors. It will be a land without leadership and without leaders. Pockets of self-government will be created or will form spontaneously, but those pockets will not extend beyond the boundaries of a village or across thoroughfares in the larger cities. The UN will have to stay to prevent these independent groups from picking up arms and doing battle again, creating the disaster of 1992 once again.

Somalia, unfortunately, is only the first of many African nations which will cease to exist as independent countries. Already we are witnessing the internationalization of government in Africa. There are seven West African nations today that are fighting a winless war in Liberia against ever-changing rebels; strife and decay are the watchword in Ethiopia, the Sudan, Ghana, Zaire, Rwanda, Burundi, Angola, Mozambique. Where starvation, mutiny, and tribal warfare are not destroying the fabric of society, illness and disease rise up to crush attempts by Africans to create a life worth living. The situation is desperate—and it will not get better. And none of the tribal, clan, or governmental warfare will equal the much greater specter of death hanging over Africa—AIDS.

By the early days of the twenty-first century, the full horror of the epidemic of AIDS will overwhelm the already fragile medical capabilities of many African states.

In Africa we have been told that AIDS—acquired immunodeficiency syndrome—is spread through sexual contact. The most affected people in the epidemic are members of the middle class. Men—clerical workers, government workers, professionals, teachers, military personnel—who have some wealth and money frequent the prostitutes of the cities. The prostitutes are legion in the big cities of central Africa where prostitution is considered a time-honored method for a young woman to earn money before she returns to her home or village to marry and raise a family.

But it is the prostitutes and the men who frequent the prostitutes who have become infected with AIDS and are spreading that disease to their wives and girlfriends and other prostitutes and their customers. The poor peasants and farmers who have no free money and who cannot travel to the major cities are the ones unaffected by the spread of AIDS through sexual intercourse.

Unfortunately, these people are not going to escape AIDS, either. About 2005, an international commission will admit that AIDS in Africa is not primarily a sexually transmitted disease—although sexual contact is a vector for spread of the deadly illness. The real culprit will be determined to be the health care delivery system. Because it is too costly to use disposable needles, and medical care is too primitive in certain hospitals, thousands of Africans will be infected with AIDS through tainted needles and syringes.

We will discover that about half the time people—men, women, and children—were being inoculated against some killer disease, they were also being infected by the incurable AIDS virus. Again circumstance will dictate that those with the most resources, the relatively wealthy middle class of Africa which can afford medical care, will be most affected by AIDS.

We will also realize that much of the spread of AIDS in Africa will come from a tainted, AIDS-infected blood supply. Since the cost of testing the blood supply for AIDS would wipe out the health budgets of cash-strapped governments in Africa, the blood is not tested. Yet it has been estimated that 10 percent or more of the supply is infected with HIV—the virus that causes AIDS. Again it is the middle class of Africans that has access to medical help and the blood supply. The disease will spread through this vector, lying dormant for years while the infected—wealthy—middle class continues to frequent prostitutes and engage in casual sex with regular partners and spouses.

Early in the twenty-first century, perhaps as early as 2002 or 2003, the full brunt of AIDS will come crashing down on sub-Saharan Africa. The middle-class population will first be hospitalized and then will die. Virtually all the educated, affluent, business, and professional classes of major cities will cease to exist. The people who make the city run, the businessmen who provide manufacturing and service jobs will die, creating loss of jobs and loss of national income; the clerical elite who pay the workers, who teach the schools, who arm the country will disappear; entire national budgets will go to pay for health care for the sick and dying; schools will cease to be used to teach, but will instead be used as makeshift hospitals as the number of people falling ill to AIDS grows geometrically.

With the productive class dead or dying, with teachers, doctors, and nurses succumbing to the same scourge that befalls their students and patients, chaos will become inevitable and the same sort of clan territorial fighting that created the disaster in Somalia will sweep across Africa.

AIDS and the collapse of government will result in the depopulation of major cities of Africa. Those crossroads of the interior will simply be given up. River dikes will not be tended and city areas will flood—not that there will be anyone around to protest or care. The jungle will reclaim vast cities. Towns will vanish without traces as the rain forest reclaims the fragile works of man. We will see firsthand what happened to the Mayas as the junglization of communities takes place in Africa. Archeologists in the late twenty-first century, around 2085, will astound the world by claiming the rediscovery of cities such as Stanleyville—cities lost to the world for generations.

The loss of the educated and professional elite will disrupt communications; roads, bridges, and rail services will falter as it becomes more and more difficult to find

healthy people to supervise or even to work at keeping
machinery working. Electricity and power facilities will
cease to function; gasoline will become nonexistent even
in countries that produce vast amounts of petroleum;
cars and buses will break down and will be abandoned
along the roads. Business will disappear, currency will
be valueless, government will not function, civilization
will disappear. Weapons will become the coin of the
realm—the realm of chaos.

The world of nations will be faced with two choices—
let Africa die or fly the blue and white flag of the United
Nations over vast territories. In my vision, I see a map
of Africa around 2010, and on that map several nations
are covered in blue.

Somalia will one day be called the savior of Africa.
Not because of anything that Somalis will do to help the
rest of the people of Africa, but because it is in Somalia
that the UN and the nations of the world finally overcame the fear of being looked upon as neo-colonists.
For the UN to intercede in Somalia, the nations of the
world, some of which had fought for independence from
European colonizers for decades, were forced to admit
that the native populations of certain parts of Africa
had utterly failed in their attempt to govern themselves.
Reluctantly, the UN took over that function for Somalia.
The coalition in West Africa was doing the same in
Liberia. The breakthrough in these countries pointed the
way for the UN to step in again, and in the twenty-first
century, the need for UN intervention will occur again
and again and again.

The map I saw showed the UN flag flying over
what was Zaire (before that the Belgian Congo), over
Mozambique, over Angola, over Tanzania, over Burkino
Faso, over Ghana, over Sierra Leone, over Liberia, over
Mali, over the Central African Republic, over Chad, over
the Sudan, over Ethiopia. Curiously, I felt a strange
sensation as I looked over the map and viewed the
Camerouns.

The more I concentrated on that central African nation the more unsettled I felt. Pictures of horror flowed over me; grotesque feelings of evil leaped at me. Slowly, frighteningly, a picture and meaning appeared: The entire nation will become a giant concentration camp—a camp where the desperately ill and hopelessly starving will be rounded up and quarantined—a euphemism for imprisonment—until they are dead.

By the year 2008, the ravages of AIDS will be so out of control on the African continent that draconian measures will be forced upon Africans in hopes that someone can be saved. The UN will "ask" the government of the Camerouns to be the quarantine site for all of Africa's AIDS patients. The people of the Camerouns will have no choice in the matter. The struggling government will either agree to be the homeland of death or it will become another UN-occupied land— and will still become the homeland on the crossroads to Hell.

The decision to accept the choiceless proposal will have long-term results for the people of the Camerouns. The term "Cameroun" will come to be considered akin to pariah. But the people of the Camerouns will reap ill-gotten wealth as they are employed to build, feed, and oversee the pitiful wretches who will be transported to the Camerouns to die.

In every town, village, and city in the UN-occupied nations teams of white-coated UN officials, armed with disposable needles and newly developed instant blood tests will round up citizens of the communities and test them for infection of HIV. Those who are positive will immediately be placed aboard trucks and taken by road or by ship or by air to the barracks and tent cities in the Camerouns where they will spend their final days, months, and years as the gruesome parasitic infections characteristic of AIDS destroys their bodies. Only rudimentary and palliative medical aid will be dispensed to the people in the camps.

The UN will rationalize that quarantine is the only method available to save any part of Africa. It will prove that four out of 10 Africans are infected with HIV—more than forty million men, women, and children—and will die of the disease before 2020. Gravediggers and crematoria workers in the Camerouns will become a new and wealthy elite. The Camerouns will become a haven for workers from third-world countries. Millions of other impoverished but educated Asians and South and Central Americans will come to Africa hopeful of finding employment in the rebuilding of the continent—a continent without a middle class.

Remarkably, the horrible solution to AIDS in Africa will work. It will work so well in the occupied nations that independent governments such as Zimbabwe, Malawi, and South Africa will send its countrymen who are infected to Camerouns as well. The worst-case solution will find advocates all over the world. Shiploads of AIDS patients from Southeast Asia and India and China will disembark in the Camerouns throughout the twenty-first century. The lesson of quarantine will be exported to other third-world countries where similar measures will be used to halt the epidemic before it can overwhelm society, but while the quarantining in Africa will be strictly enforced only as a measure of preventing the spread of disease, elsewhere it will be used to eliminate dissidents, grossly reminiscent of Nazi concentration camps and Soviet gulags of the mid-twentieth century.

The vision of Africa is grim, but it is not unrelenting. By the year 2050, education of a new generation of disease-free children, a new middle-class elite schooled in the concepts of democracy, and nations tragically thinned by deaths of a quarter to two-thirds of their population will emerge as powerful, democratic, resource-wealthy, and independent nations eager to shake off the yoke of benevolent occupation.

Among the amazing success stories of Africa will be Uganda. Once considered the "Pearl of the British

Empire," Uganda began a spiral to the depths of civilization during the 1970s. That saw the rise of Idi Amin and a succession of vicious strongmen who destroyed and bankrupted the nation. Of all the nations of Africa, during the 1980s and 1990s Uganda was the most affected by AIDS with upwards of 25 percent of the population infected—entire villages, 100 percent of the inhabitants, infected with HIV.

In the midst of this chaos, a new strongman, Musaveni, who armed five-year-old followers with machine guns, came to power. Most of the world rolled its eyes and awaited another reign of terror and bloodshed and hideous death to claim Uganda. But somewhere along the line the cycle of death and destruction was snapped. The children who learned how to ambush convoys before they were teenagers went back to school. The government reduced its expenditures on weaponry and invested in infrastructure and modern medicine. True, the dying due to AIDS and occasional insurrection continued, but by the year 2005, the world could see that Uganda had turned the corner.

Investment in the country, inspired by awesome scenery, mild climate, and strong, if not very democratic government, will increase dramatically. The government will encourage immigration, especially of the clerical classes that had been decimated by AIDS and a generation of internal strife. By 2010, Uganda will fully recover and will become a tourist mecca. Even democracy will rebound although the military will still hold sway, permitting politicians a certain leeway.

By the end of the twenty-first century Africa as a whole will rejoin the world as a far more civilized and modern place. But the mounds of death—created by the mass graves of those who perished through disease or warfare—will dot every city and every town throughout the continent. The chill of death and occupation will remain in the heart of every African for generations.

3

AMERICA, THE EXPANSIONIST

THE GRAPHIC IMAGERY OF DEATH AND DESTRUCTION
across Africa that I had seen in my visions overwhelmed
my fragile psyche.

I lit a cigarette to calm my nerves. I watched as
the smoke created intricate patterns within the shadows created by the late afternoon sun. It lulled me into
a false state of security.

Without warning the smoke took on another shape,
another form. At first, the forms I was seeing looked
sinister; that feeling continued as the color red flowed
across the images.

The red oozed unevenly and slowly dripped over my
viewpoint, blotting out the familiar furnishings of my
apartment. I was apprehensive as my mind assimilated
the meaning of the color. Red has meant war, blood,
death.

Already I knew of the disaster that is awaiting Africa.
I thought in horror, Can this be an omen of something
even worse?

Suddenly, the red canvas started to undulate and look more like fabric than a menace and then even that fabric began to fade—almost hidden by another force—this time a gray, rolling fog. The cloud enveloped the field of red and then my room and then it covered me as well.

No longer was I worried. I knew the fog. It always seems to arrive when it's time for me to discover the future. I breathed deeply and peered into the mist—and through the damp I could see a field of stars, hundreds of stars.

Curiously, the stars were not bright white lights against a stark background of black, as they look on a cold clear winter's night in the countryside. These stars appeared on a field of blue.

I peered through the fog to try to understand if this was a clue to the future. Surrounding the stars, I now could see twinkling lights that appeared in folds. The Northern Lights—aurora borealis, I thought. There were tremendous folds of bright red, and other folds of white, flowing as if being blown by a gentle but firm breeze.

Slowly, understanding began to penetrate my consciousness. I was not seeing a phenomenon of the heavens, I was looking at the future—the future of a vastly expanded United States of America.

As I concentrated on the image that was rapidly focusing in my mind, understanding grew, explanations arose, and a glorious future for this country—and most likely a frightening scenario for many other nations—unfolded in my automatic writings.

The admission of Puerto Rico as the fifty-first state at the turn of the century will give impetus to a neo-nationalistic, imperialistic drive in the United States, but events that have little to do with expansionism will nevertheless power the expansion of the country.

The collapse of communism in Cuba will lead to repatriation of tens of thousands of Cuban-Americans to their homeland, just ninety miles south of Key West.

These re-settlers will return to Cuba with honed business skills and will almost overnight become a new upper class in Cuba. They will open cabarets, restaurants, factories, and retail establishments with speed and success that will dazzle the Cubans who have wandered the barren fields of communism for forty years.

But along with the skills that make them shrewd and successful businessmen, these returning Cubans will bring with them a new product—American-style democracy. They will become frustrated, angry, and desperate as they see the corruption of the remnants of Castro's Cuba threaten to steal their hard-won successes.

After several major companies are regulated to death by the Cuban government, an alarmed business class will begin to agitate for unification with the United States. The hundreds of thousands of second- and third-generation Cuban-Americans living in the United States will hear the voice of their kinsmen on Cuba and will amplify that sound.

By 2012, the noise will be deafening. Pro-Cuban statehood on the mainland will be a major political party platform, with historians pointing out that if the United States had acted on a previous statehood movement for Cuba—100 years earlier in the early 1900s— a century of chaos for both Cuba and the United States would have been eliminated. There would have been no Cuban missile crisis, there would have been no Cuban boatlift immigrations, there would have been no Castro and no communism a cheap plane ride away from the United States coast.

On Cuba itself, the push for statehood will have to fight a barely functioning government and fading nationalism. Votes will be forced on the government to accept statehood, and the votes will lose—but the margins of defeat will be less and less. Soldiers backing the government, fearful of losing privileges if the country becomes a state, will try to stop another vote in 2015 that seems likely to win. The coup attempt will last for a matter of days, during which time US warships will blockade the island.

The Cuban troops will give up, and an interim government will hold the elections that will ask for US statehood. Congress will quickly approve the request.

While the turmoil in Cuba is leading toward statehood, another scenario will be developing in Costa Rica. The democratic and financially stable government of Central America will become a haven for tourists and retired Americans in the later quarter of the twentieth century. Costa Rica offers beautiful beaches, primitive jungles, sophisticated entertainment, and primitive art within a remarkably small nation.

The government exists without an army and without fear of internal or external enemies. It has a stable economy, based mainly on tourism and exports of fruits and vegetables. All these attributes will combine to end its function as an independent nation.

As the cost of living escalates in the United States and the benefits to the elderly in the US are reduced due to budget constraints that will follow the Clinton administration, Costa Rica will become a haven for retired Americans.

With their income—still far greater than the income of a middle-class Costa Rican—the elderly will buy homes and set up retirement communities from the Caribbean coast of the nation, across the country's interior and mountainous spine and down to the Pacific Ocean. Thousands of Americans will migrate to Costa Rica each year. Tourism will swell as the relatives of these transplanted Americans visit their parents' adopted land, bringing untold prosperity to the entire country.

In 2019, however, the dreams, prosperity, and independence of Costa Rica will be changed by the will of nature. A massive, slow-moving hurricane with winds of 130 miles per hour will churn across the Caribbean and crush the east coast of the country. Damage will be overwhelming. While the east coast is devastated by winds and rain, the west coast of the nation will suffer from devastating floods, mudslides, and horrendous pounding waves that will damage and destroy docks and air facilities.

In the space of two days, the idyllic nature of the nation will be history. The families of Americans living in Costa Rica will demand in the name of humanity that the American government aid the beleaguered Costa Ricans and the Americans living there. Aware of criticism that it hadn't acted fast enough when other natural disasters struck, the US government will fly in plane after plane of supplies and soldiers to control looting and homeless mobs.

The devastation will be so great that American relief and police forces will spend months in the nation. The government of Costa Rica, unable to handle the catastrophe of the storm by itself, will meekly watch as everyday operation of the country is taken over by Americans. A year later it will be obvious to all that Costa Rica has ceased to function as an independent state. Feeble attempts to maintain independent status will be ignored. American pressure will force the Costa Rican legislature to offer citizenship to Americans living in the country—citizens who will opt for statehood within three years.

Meanwhile, changes along the Mexican–United States border will become ugly. Again business will rule the future. The passage of the North American Free Trade Association treaty by Mexico, the United States, and Canada will be the cause of further US expansion.

The prediction of H. Ross Perot in the 1992 presidential race that "there will be a great sucking noise of jobs going south" once the treaty is approved will be confirmed.

But while it will be the jobs that are going south, it will be mainly Americans or Mexican-Americans who will be given most of those jobs. Major corporations will set up factory after factory along the border between Mexico and the United States. Mexico will lack many of the skilled laborers needed to run the factories and thousands of Americans will follow the jobs across the border—and make Mexico prosper. Interestingly, economists will be pleased to find that as many jobs go south, the work pool in the United States will decrease but become more skilled. Prosperity in Mexico will also bolster prosperity across the border as well.

As the job force develops in Mexico, more and more Americans will emigrate there, making the resorts on the Gulf of California the new "in" place; on the opposite shore of the scenic arm of the Pacific, tourists will swamp Baja California. In the factory communities, labor organizers will begin to seek rudimentary unions.

With more Americans will come more news of Americans in Mexico—and news of abuses by the traditionally underpaid police forces who have for decades devised creative forms of revenue enhancement—usually at the expense and sometimes at the lives of Americans. Tourists will be threatened, the families of factory workers will be terrorized, union leaders will be lynched. The authorities will seem helpless to bring the guilty to justice.

Faster than someone can say "Remember the Alamo," the new citizens who are working in northern Mexico or pumping oil at Veracruz or are at play in Baja, Tijuana, or Puerto Vallarta will demand that something be done about the atrocities being committed. Among the ideas suggested will be to send in the marines—the US Marines. The response of an arrogant, wealthy, and distant government in Mexico City will be to send in Mexican troops with orders to end the disturbances. In 2024, in a confrontation in Nogales, Mexico, across the border from Nogales, Arizona, a group of angry union members will walk off the job in a wildcat strike. They will prevent automobile workers from crossing the picket lines. The governor of the Mexican state of Sonora will send soldiers to the factory with orders to disperse the mob; the Mexican federal government will seal the border despite the protest of the United States.

As Americans watch from rooftops in Nogales across the fence which separates the two nations, they see Mexican soldiers fire at the strikers. A dozen men and women fall into the dusty land. From the American side, a private citizen fires his own long range rifle at the soldiers, slightly wounding one of them. The soldiers turn and fire back across the border, killing one American and riddling dozens of buildings with bullets.

In Phoenix, the governor of Arizona orders state troopers to fly SWAT team helicopters to the Mexican side of the border and pick up the dead and wounded. Mexico warns that such an attempt will be met by force. A panicked and outraged administration in Washington backs the governor's action and sends a squadron of combat helicopters from New Mexico to "assist" the SWAT teams. When one of the SWAT team helicopters is shot down, the US Army copters decimate the Mexican troops on the ground and a squadron of US troops secure the town.

With tensions reaching a fever pitch, a wild card is thrown into the conflict. In a coordinated assault, people living in San Jose de Cabo, at the tip of Baja California, and others in Tijuana, Mexicali, and Ensenada take over the local broadcast systems, declare the independence of Baja California from Mexico, and immediately request annexation by the United States. While many of the people in the assault are Americans, the vast majority are Mexicans who believe that their fate, future, and fortunes will be better if they cut ties to Mexico.

As Americans and Mexican forces tensely face each other around Nogales, the situation escalates. About two hundred US Marines from San Diego take positions along the mouth of the Colorado River, roughly the border of the Mexican states of Baja California Norte and Sonora; committees of the US House and Senate approve the annexation request of Baja California and

US Coast Guard cutters and hydrofoil attack craft patrol the Gulf of California.

Complications increase as tourist-conscious Yucatan declares that its citizens—mostly descendants of Mayan Indians—also want to be free of the corrupt and ineffectual government of Mexico City. The request for US military protection is approved by the US which sends thousands of troops across the Yucatan Straits from Cuba. Revolts against the central government—some by natives such as those in Merida on the Yucatan which are joined by nearby Cancun expatriated Americans—occur in Monterrey, Veracruz, and Acapulco. The Mexican government collapses in disarray; attempts by military leaders fail to bring the revolution under control. The best the military can do is create pockets of territorial holdings of citizens who are either loyal to Mexico or are too afraid to resist the warlords.

United States troops are called in by local rebellious authorities who, once under the protection of American soldiers, request annexation as states. With statehood fever burning strongly, Congress quickly agrees to admit four different sections of Mexico as states: Baja California and a section of coastal Mexico on the opposite shore of the Gulf of California become state fifty-three; huge sections of Sonora, Chihuahua, Coahuila, and Nuevo León (Monterrey) become state fifty-four; the Yucatan and the coast territory along the Caribbean, which includes the important seaport of Veracruz, are accepted as state fifty-five; and the territory along the Pacific shore, including Acapulco, is admitted a year later in 2032 as the fifty-sixth state. Independent Mexico is reduced to a small area along the Pacific intermountain desert which includes Durango and Mexico City and its environs.

The stunning growth of the United States continues to the north where Canada is coming apart at the seams about 2030. The industrious, wealthy, resource-rich, French-speaking province of Quebec demands so

much favored-province status that the other provinces
determine to abandon the commonwealth.

First to jump ship are the maritime provinces of New
Brunswick, Nova Scotia, Prince Edward Island, and
Labrador. The four provinces on the eastern seaboard
seek admission as one state—a request that is backed
by the New England States and is approved quickly.

Then British Columbia and the Yukon Territory ask
for admission as a single-state entity, which gives the
United States an uninterrupted border from the Arctic
Circle to the Yucatan Peninsula.

The Canadian prairie provinces of Alberta, Saskatchewan, and Manitoba follow quickly behind the maritime
and the western provinces, eager to combine their cattle and grain-producing merchandise in the general US
hopper.

Ontario accedes to the US Constitution after several years of trying to make Canada work as a nation
in partnership with Quebec. But the uncompromising
Quebecois make the union untenable for the most populous of the provinces. Ontario divorces from Quebec
and joins in marriage with the US and puts the entire
Great Lakes system into the hands of the United States
of America.

Of the original Canadian federation at the start of
the twenty-first century only the sparsely settled Northwest Territories and Quebec remain. The federal city of
Ottawa remains with what's left of Canada, which now
changes its name to Quebec Republic.

The first action of the republic is to nearly go to war
with the United States over the matter of a boundary
with Labrador. The boundary between the two provinces has been unsettled since the nineteenth century.
Tensions are high between the two nations, but a peace-
seeking Washington administration finally strikes a bargain with the Quebecois.

In return for free use of the St. Lawrence River,
which passes through Quebec to the Atlantic Ocean—

a lifeline for Great Lakes traffic—the US gives up large portions of Labrador, mainly land which has few inhabitants, but may contain tremendous mineral assets.

By the third quarter of the twenty-first century there are sixty-five United States of America, and the red, white, and blue flag covers every territory in the Caribbean and in North and Central America except a few tiny islands, Quebec, the slice of Mexico, and Guatemala, which successfully bucked the tide of American nationalism and expansionism.

4

THE GUIDE

I WAS WIDE AWAKE AND FROZEN BY FEAR.

I had this anticipatory feeling in the pit of my stomach that something dreadful was about to occur.

A click. My microwave oven let out a distressed beep. I knew the electricity had gone out. Goosebumps arose on my arms and legs.

I tried to make my mind work. Maybe, I thought, I'm really asleep and I'm dreaming? But even as I thought that I knew that whatever had awakened me was no dream.

In the darkness I could sense a mysterious, dark shape. I could almost feel the pupils in my eyes dilate, desperately trying to find enough faint light to reveal what the presence was that seemed to be be hovering near me.

Every New Yorker has some idea of what she'll do if she ever comes face to face with a burglar or robber. I know that I used to have a plan, too. Whatever that plan was, however, I had no idea at this moment. I was just simply terrified.

Now the shape added definition. I could see a body, a head; I sensed maleness. There's a strange man in my room! I thought in panic. And as my eyes widened, I thought I could see details of his face, but all I could really see was the black glint of light that flickered off his eyes—eyes that seemed malevolently large and fearfully close to my own.

My terror was complete. I thought, If I scream will anyone hear me? If I scream and anyone hears me will anyone care? If someone hears me and cares, will they act—and will they act soon enough to keep this intruder from killing me? I was amazed at how much one could think in the space of just a few beats of my panicked heart.

Then came the voice. I couldn't be certain that his lips moved, but his voice was clear. So clear it seemed as if he had spoken directly to my mind, bypassing my ears.

"So, you can see me," he said. It was a statement, not a question. "You are afraid. Perhaps you should be, but you knew I was coming.

"There is no reason to fear me," he said. "I am here because you need me. You have been calling me for help for months—and you know why."

I didn't know why, at least I didn't think I knew why.

He stared at me. Immediately I saw a statue. An Indian maiden. Of course, the shrine at Auriesville.

"Yes, you saw Kateri Tekakwitha's statue. You knelt before the Lily of the Mohawks. That's where you saw the visions and the light and mysteries which you can't unlock by yourself."

My God, I thought. The visions. That's what this is all about. But then, I wondered, How in the world does he know that? And what in the world is he doing here?

My imagination ran wild. Is this person for real? Am I just imagining this? Is he just a specter of the future— or of the past?

He answered my thoughts. "What I am is what you decide I am. But I am real enough. If you hear me, you will know why I'm here, why you are here, and what the vision means. But you should know that you aren't the only person to have seen these visions. Many others have seen them in this time and before."

I was mesmerized. I didn't say a word. And whoever it was continued. "Kateri saw the visions of the future much the way you did. She accepted that people can see things they can't explain. She knew that someday she would be able to explain what the visions meant to her. But she knew instinctively that the people she lived with, the Mohawks, might view such revelations with disdain or worse—even though Native Americans easily accepted the notion of predictive visions.

"The great Iroquois chief Hiawatha, in fact, believed so much in the visions of one of his shamans that Hiawatha created the incredibly successful Iroquois confederacy long before democracy reared its ugly head in the New World."

I gazed upon the man's face, aglow with pride and accomplishment. "So," I assumed, "you are that shaman, medicine man, the visionary that talked to Hiawatha?"

He spoke to me again, and again it was in that same mysterious voice that was heard in my head. I could now see him clearly enough to realize that I was looking at a figure, not unlike a hologram, that had very small movements. I even suspected that the movements I saw—in his eyes and where his chest seemed to heave as if he were breathing—were artifacts of my own attempts to make sense of the unbelievable.

He said, "Your assumption is wrong. I helped that shaman interpret the messages he received from the Greatest Spirit of all. There have been different names given to the Greatest Spirit. Every group has referred to him in some manner and to every group he has offered a chance to develop a prosperous and thriving community. When it seems as if that community is heading to a spiral of destruction, the Greatest Spirit has sent his warnings to the world.

"These warnings are received by thousands of people and are rejected by virtually all of them. And so their races disappear through famine or warfare or failing to heed the warnings of natural disasters. It happens over and over again. Fortunately sometimes a person comes along who will listen to the warnings and will interpret them correctly. Others are fortunate enough to have the spiritual wisdom to accept help—that's me."

A thousand questions came to me at once. I knew there was a trap in accepting this individual at his word. Even in dealing with psychic phenomena all my life, I knew too well that some of the messages sent to the quick from the dead are not all beneficial. There is an oozing, pus-filled black side of the psychic world, too. Often that which seems to be the best is in truth the worst that can happen.

"Why have you been sent here?" I asked. "Why me? Why do you even care what we mortal souls do, if you are immortal?"

The man stepped back and held his hands up as if to ward off an assault. A grim smile appeared on his face. "See, I have the power to move and respond," he said, answering the question I hadn't even formed in my mind. "The easiest question to answer is the last one you asked. Why do we immortals take the time to trifle with you who struggle to breathe your own polluted air when the air we breathe in our world is pure and fresh?

"As much as we here would not care to admit it, without you we are nothing. Those of you who believe in us devoutly and those of you who believe in us profanely and those of you who believe in us not at all create our existence. Without you we are truly nothingness. Our immortal existence would exist for no purpose. There would be eternal nothingness and we would simply fade away.

"We believe that we are helping mankind reach a higher level of existence by making sure that mankind does exist and does not destroy himself or his planet. We gave man the ability to think and build and invent on his own. We knew that he would stumble on the path to greatness and that we would be able to shift him on to the correct path. What we didn't realize until late in what you call the nineteenth century was that we had done too well. That man had decided that science, mathematics, archaeology, and other sciences held all the answers. Mankind was discouraged—even tortured and killed—for suggesting that an individual could be a prophet. We should have known from the past but even spirits often have higher expectations than are warranted.

"Look through the ages. Remember the story of Noah. He understood what we were trying to tell him and through the forcefulness of his own character he convinced his sons and family to build this huge boat in the middle of land. Noah knew the storm was coming and his family accepted that Noah had this vision. Those who mocked him died. They drowned not because they ridiculed Noah but because they did not accept that predictions were possible and were meaningful.

"There have been hundreds of prophets through the ages and some of the most receptive of the prophets refused to take their service. Look up the story of Jonah, one of the greatest malcontents as a prophet we ever had to work with. Jonah was told to go to the great city of Nineveh and proclaim the coming of the end, that the spirit world was going to destroy the city because of its evil ways.

"What did Jonah do: He hopped on a ship going in the opposite direction. So we had to retrieve him, creating a majestic storm that only ended when his shipmates—hearing of his refusal to do the work of a prophet—flung him overboard. Jonah was driving us crazy: Here's a guy who shrinks from our service on a mission to save tens of thousands of lives; but he's willing to spare the lives of fifty shipmates he's never seen before by admitting that he's running away.

"So into the water goes Jonah and the sea settles down, the storm subsides. We found a huge fish—no it's not a whale, but that's what happens when the story gets retold—which swallows Jonah whole and spits him out on dry land (anyway that's the way Jonah explains why he was late getting to Nineveh. It's a good tale, and we shouldn't corrupt it any further).

"Jonah goes to Nineveh and starts proclaiming the end of the world. He is so convincing in his tale of prophecy—and remember this is being done reluctantly—that the people believe him. They take off their jewels and fine clothes—everyone including the king—and repent. The catastrophe passes. The city is saved.

"And what is Jonah's reaction? He complains. 'What good is being a prophet if you prophesize something and it doesn't come true?' Jonah would have been happier if one hundred thousand people would have died."

He looked at me curiously. "If you turn out to be another Jonah, I will kill you the way you thought I was going to when you first saw me." He smiled, but somehow I knew he wasn't joking.

He sat down on the bed. I was stunned to realize that he wasn't just a vision. The bed rocked gently as he rested upon it. I started to say something, but he raised his arm to silence me.

"Let me continue. You should know this before we go on. There have been other prophets who have failed to deliver the message clearly. You are familiar with Nostradamus. Here is a man who received the messages from the Greatest Spirit much the way you did. As you know Nostradamus recognized the psychic import of the words, auras, and visions.

"We came to assist him in interpreting the messages, but he rejected us. 'I can see the messages for myself, I don't know if you are an angel or a demon. I will choose how to tell the world what the world must know.' People have spent four hundred years trying to figure out what Nostradamus was saying. By the time they have a clue the event has happened and any attempt to try to prevent the catastrophe has passed.

"It's a good thing I wasn't his guide—oh yes, there are many of us—or I would have slaughtered him on the spot, much the way the Mohawks at Ossernenon wiped out priests before the arrival of Kateri."

He looked at me sternly. "Shawn, you may ignore me and ignore the messages. You may say that you aren't interested in helping your fellow man. You may claim like Jonah that you aren't strong enough or willing enough to be a prophet. These possibilities we accept. But don't believe that you can interpret these images by yourself. You need the help we can offer. If you plan to tell the world what is going to happen in the future, let us assist. An error in interpretation could be the ruination of mankind."

I shook my head in awe. "Of course, I would let you help me. I've been going crazy trying to figure these things out. I haven't slept well in months knowing that what you have given to me is important and having so much difficulty in sorting it all out. You are an answer to my prayers."

He stood again. "And yet you wonder why you have been chosen." I nodded. "You should know that even today people go to pray and contemplate the feats of Kateri Tekakwitha at Auriesville and receive the same messages that you receive. But rarely does anyone understand what is happening. They'll say, 'What a wonderful, calm place. I feel uplifted. I feel strange. I feel as if some power has gone through me.' They'll take the medals and holy water back with them and will rub the relic of Kateri and assume that their faith is being revived. Basically, they don't get it.

"There are others that receive the message and understand that something special has happened to them, but they will not know how to proceed. Eventually the message, the light, the aura will vanish from their minds.

A vision is a very perishable commodity. It has to be turned into something hard and fast—such as a writing—before it floats away on the same breeze that brought it. And even those who attempt to put into words what happened to them will still fail because they will not be able to perceive us.

"It's interesting, of course, to see the works of humans, especially the artistry of the motion picture as it has developed during the twentieth century. We frankly are in love with the movies. Since we can control our time, we get to see them all—without shirking our own duties. In my world, we love the idea of the movie *Beetlejuice* in which the young couple are killed and become ghosts in their own home. What we find interesting is the concept that the new buyers of the home cannot see the ghosts—but their child can. It's not that they can't see the ghosts, it's that they don't want to see them.

"When you, Shawn, saw my face in the visions, you wanted to see me. Sometimes your own natural feelings got in the way and sent you off on tangents that didn't make sense. But I was always there waiting, hoping that you would finally be able to see me with your mind as well as with your eyes and with your touch."

He put his hand on mine. The touch was electric.

"I am real, you see," he told me, "and I'm here to help. I can show you the most wonderful things and some of the most awful things. We ask in return that all you do is to try to warn people. The end of the twentieth century is not a good time for prophets or predictions. You could be mocked or called an alarmist or denounced or even have your life threatened by zealots for other causes. We will understand if you deny us, but we implore you to try. There are so few people who understand the messages and are in a position to interpret them. You are one of them. We beseech you to do the right thing. If you do decide, I will help you as best I can for as long as I can. There are others who need our help. We never can have enough people to help. We never do have enough."

His request was simple enough to answer. I had always intended to try to write something about what I was seeing. I knew its importance and I wasn't afraid of being scoffed at or looked down upon. I've had nearly fifty years of dealing with people who just wouldn't believe or simply don't care to believe.

"Yes, I will try to do what I can to warn the world," I told him. "But, if I am to work with you, you must at least tell me your name or what I can call you."

He arched his eyebrows. "My name. My name to you would be unpronounceable. There are many syllables and they are from a tongue as foreign to you as English is to a native of the Amazon rain forest. You don't have to call me by name. Just call me what I am and what I will be to you, 'Guide.' "

5

NEW JOBS/TECHNOLOGY

THE EARLY MORNING SUN STREAMED INTO THE APART-
ment. The noise of the city streets rumbled through the
windows.

I sat stunned, unmoving, not knowing what I should
do next.

"Let's go outside," the Guide said. I felt pale, shaken,
closed in. I could use the fresh air, I thought.

We went outside and I knew that I was supposed to
hail a cab. I knew we were going to Wall Street. I
couldn't understand why, because Wall Street is empty
on Sunday—especially Sunday morning.

We got out at Wall Street after a silent ride downtown. I knew that the cabdriver couldn't see the Guide
and I didn't want the cabby to wonder about my mental
health by having a conversation with a phantom.

Once on the streets of New York, no one thought twice
about someone having an animated discussion with someone who wasn't there. In fact, as we walked through the
shadows of the World Trade Center and other bastions
of finance, a couple of down-and-out and unsteady-on-
their feet passersby nodded to me as if they understood
my problems. Others bid hello to the Guide. "Can they

see you, too?" I asked, my mouth sagging open.

"I don't know," the Guide said, craning his head around to look at one derelict, who promptly waved at him. My mysterious apparition truly seemed shaken by the experience. "Maybe . . . maybe."

We strolled along Wall Street and peered over at the strangely silent Stock Exchange. "On a weekday, this place literally vibrates with activity," I told him.

"Yes, I know. But today we are really looking at the future."

I looked at him closely. I had my notebook of writings with me and I thumbed through it trying to locate clues. I was looking for information about a major monetary crisis: A disaster so profound that the financial heart of the world stopped beating. But nothing appeared in the book that could relate to some type of financial Black Monday that heralded the Great Depression. I found some "$$$$" markings and a couple of squiggles.

I stopped in the middle of the street, unafraid of traffic, which was virtually nonexistent today. The breeze through the metal and stone canyons whipped up a few papers and wafted them through the air and around my feet. I showed the Guide what I had written. "Is this what you meant?" I asked him. "Do these symbols point to the demise of Wall Street?"

He put a hand on my shoulder. "Relax, Shawn," he said. "You are getting your images mixed. Yes, those symbols refer to what I'm talking about—but your conclusions and your fears are wrong."

We walked out of harm's way and found a bench to rest on. He swept his arm across the near-deserted streets and began to explain why the future of Wall Street was silence.

First, he began with a history lesson. "Four hundred years ago this street was called Wall Street. Why? Because this was where the Dutch built walls to protect New Amsterdam from attack. Wall Street became the center of commerce as New Amsterdam became New

York and the Dutch colony became British and then became the capital of the United States and then the financial center of this country and the world."

Wall Street had indeed changed from one use to another in its relatively short history. It will become something else again because this entire world—especially the idea of buying and selling stocks—is going to change remarkably in the next century.

"Shawn," he said. "Don't let your nephews or your friends' kids grow up to be stockbrokers. It's a profession that will not exist by the year 2025."

By 2025, the telecommunications highway will run through every home with electricity and create the computer power that will allow anyone who wants stocks to buy them themselves—without having to pay the commissions now charged by brokers. If you want a stock, you'll simply punch into the computer a request for information about the company and your facsimile printer will spew out all the relevant data. Then you make the purchase directly from the company or directly from other individuals willing to sell the stock at the price you are asking. You'll bargain and negotiate directly with others who hold the company's paper. You won't have to sell or buy on an exchange or through members of that exchange.

Of course, Wall Street fought the new arrangements tooth and nail, but the fight was one-sided and over quickly. Stockbrokers discarded their careers and became stock information specialists, selling their expertise to the myriad companies that supply stock information to sellers and buyers of stocks.

Once a person made a decision to purchase a stock or a bond, the transaction was handled automatically and instantaneously. His bank account was debited the proper amount for the transaction, and the stock was registered to his name.

The need for a stockbroker was obviated.

I let my eyes wander up from the street to the doors of the exchange and over its distinctive architecture. I wondered what would become of this and other citadels of finance. The Guide answered before I could put my thoughts into speech.

"Museums. Restaurants. Schools. One of the truly magnificent restaurants of the mid-twenty-first century will take over the New York Stock Exchange building. The upscale delicatessen will feature some delightful sandwiches named after defunct geography in the building. My favorite is a huge tongue, roast beef and turkey on rye sandwich—one could have fed most of Kateri Tekakwitha's long house—which will be called the 'Trading Floor,' " he said.

People still will come to Wall Street but no longer to look for a financial windfall. Instead, artists are to be drawn to the architecture; young lovers to be drawn to the museums and restaurants. Entrepreneurs will create magnificent condos in the offices that used to house legions of stockbrokers and commercial lawyers. Wall Street will evolve into another role—New York's best-loved Bohemian center, a beckon to the world's artists, authors, sculptors, and poets.

As the Guide rambled on about how Wall Street would change, I wondered how the country would pay for everyone to be hooked up to the electronic communication highway.

"That's an interesting question," he said. "Look in your notebook." He took it from me and leafed through the pages, now getting worn and frayed. Surreptitiously, I looked around to see if anyone was gawking at us. I expected to see a dozen people staring at me and pointing to the notebook that was hovering in mid-air. But this is New York City. If anyone among the few people on the street did notice, no one glanced twice.

"Here," he said, drawing me to his side. "You've written 'Electric War.' What do you think that means?" I closed my eyes and tried to let images appear in my head but before I could try to decipher anything the Guide cut me off.

"It's too bizarre. If you could conjure up the events of the Electric War you would discard them as being too farfetched. But it happened; it was strange, but it was true. The Electric War occurred in central Alabama in 2032 because one community attempted to put up road-blocks on the communications highway," he explained.

The fundamental church and government leaders of the county decided that the communications highway was some sort of international plot designed to destroy America, religion, and "God's law." The powerful politi-cal leaders—empowered by 58 percent of the vote in the county—refused to allow the community to be wired for the communications highway.

By this time, it was generally assumed that just about every household in the country that had elec-tricity had direct communications with business, arts, science, schools, news organizations, etc. That wasn't because everyone scrimped and saved to pay for the latest hardware from IBM or software from Microsoft. Once business realized what a powerful advantage it was to have people—i.e., consumers—wired to their catalogs and stores, big business paid households to install the cameras, computers, and modems that connected every-one to everything. And if something new came out, the companies made sure that every home was given the latest model. Some companies even paid subscribers to tune into its network at least a couple of hours a week so it could showcase new wares.

Everywhere the communications highway was paved, everyone prospered—even despite computer hacking that kept business and police on their toes. Gener-ally it worked and worked well—except in Central Alabama.

The war broke out when a family living on the border of a county that had communications highway technol-ogy spent its own money to run the necessary cables across the county line to hook up to the twenty-first century. When one of the children blurted out in school about how wonderful it was to get all this new information, he was reported by school teachers to county officials. The county dispatched its police force to take the equipment out of the home, but the police were met by a group of about one hundred men, women, and children—part of the minority that wanted their community to benefit from the technology that was revolutionizing the way Americans lived in the twenty-first century.

Stymied by the crowd, and not expecting any organized resistance, the sheriff's deputies retreated. County officials tried to cut off electricity to the home, but the stubborn family, now being assisted openly by friends and discreetly by corporate giants, set up portable, wind-powered generators and satellite dishes to stay connected. Clandestine cables were laid at night to other homes nearby and soon dozens of families were on the communications highway.

The 'war' escalated when mobs led by the keep-'em-out-of-my-backyard officials broke into the homes where the computer systems were up and running and destroyed the machinery and generally wrecked the houses. Several of the homeowners were injured by the invaders, but many of the home invaders suffered injuries as well. Of course, the entire episode was recorded by dozens of newsmen who were watching the story unfold and when deputies were identified as being among the people involved, the state government took action against the county. The sheriff was ousted by the governor; all the deputies and local police officials were relieved of arrest powers as state troopers took over local law enforcement. The camcorders produced enough clear identifications of the home invaders that the homeowners were able to sue for damages.

Faced with financial ruin and the sincere chance of serving time in jail in federal prison ranches in Montana, the effort to prevent the highway from coming to their homes was abandoned. The "war" was over. The "war" was startling to much of America. Although the bloody battles were confined to Alabama, Americans and the world soon learned that this wasn't the only place where technology had to fight to be believed. Hundreds of holdouts protested against paving their living rooms with the communications highway. But the Alabama case was the largest attempt by any form of government in the United States to control the bulldozer of progress. Technology had won, allowing all its promise—both good and bad—to become universal.

The impact of how the communications highway was reshaping America is illustrated by the question of sex education. Now instead of just asking Mom and Dad for facts on the birds and the bees—or more likely going down to the levee and discussing sex with peers who often knew very little more than what big brothers or big sisters had told them—the whole family could discuss the subject with experts in the field.

And if the subject was too embarrassing for the parents—and the kids—it could be approached individually. The proponents of the communications highway saw most of the pitfalls before they occurred. Questions about sex and other controversial topics of the day—interestingly, sex has always been one of the controversial topics of the day and the advent of a new century won't change that a bit—required permission of the adult.

If a child asked the computer to explain where babies come from and how they are made, the computer would ascertain the child's age, ask if the child has received parental permission to discuss the subject (parental coding would be demanded), and would then hook the child up to either a written discussion of the subject or a live connection with either governmental or private consultants or therapists—again with parental consent. The computer or the live specialist would answer questions as the young minds presented them, taking care not to delve beyond the child's ability to comprehend.

For more difficult questions, including the proper time for sexual intercourse or even whether it was right to carry a baby to term or have an adoption, the computer would present several authorities with differing viewpoints to discuss the pros and cons, ethically, morally, religiously, and pragmatically.

One of the great benefits of the communications highway was to remove many questions of life and morality from the school curriculums, allowing schools to return to fundamentals of reading, writing, arithmetic, and computer interfacing.

On the down side of the communications highway, however, were numerous cases of computer interface overload. People would become so enamored of their ability to ask questions and receive information on virtually any subject any time of day or night that they became almost glued to their computers. They made couch potatoes look like aerobic instructors. There were incredible cases of people who ate, slept, and even defecated in front of their computers because they didn't dare leave the machines for fear they would miss something that would change their lives. There were even cases in which people starved to death by working so long at their computers they forgot to eat; some people collapsed and died of heart rhythm dysfunctions because they had gone ten to twelve days without sleep.

Although these cases were few and far between, the federal authorities required that time governors be placed on all the communications highway equipment—shutting the system down for six hours if it was not turned off during the previous seventy-two hour period. In case of national or international emergencies, however, the ban was lifted so that people could watch CNN report history as it was occurring.

The communications highway technology spawned a number of new jobs. One that became a favorite of kids who still wanted to drop out of high school and/or college was "Fax repair specialist." With information the most fascinating thing to obtain at home every night, there had to be a way to record it. Businesses also demanded a way of making sure their advertisements remained in front of their customers. The facsimile machines hummed all day and all night, and no matter how simply they were designed, there were still people in the US and around the world who were hopeless in figuring out how to change the paper. Worse, sometimes the machines actually broke. Sometimes, Junior poured oatmeal into the device or the dog knocked a can of Coke into the printer. That meant you had to get more paper quickly and get the machine replaced or repaired instantly.

A young high school dropout in Seattle whose goal in life was to become the next Bill Gates (billionaire founder and president of Microsoft) borrowed from Domino's Pizza and an emergency hotline to create the 211-Line. He guaranteed that he could get your disabled or out-of-paper facsimile machine up and running in thirty minutes—and that he wouldn't charge the customer a penny (he did charge the businesses a bundle, but they loved him for it). By the year 2040, the 211-Line franchises were located in every town—and on nearly every street corner in major cities.

There is always a problem with new technology and with the facsimile explosion across America came the problem of what to do with all the fax paper that was accumulating around the world. With the ever-growing problem of where to put our garbage, the properties of facsimile paper made it difficult to recycle with other papers. Mounds of facsimile paper were piling up everywhere.

But it was discovered that by crumpling up the facsimile paper you could create a cheap and effective form of insulation that was especially useful in building structures on the Moon, the planets, and in orbiting space stations and space labs. That generated another new field—the fax recycling agent. Collectors would actually go door to door and bid for people's used faxes. The more fax paper you threw into special bins, the more you were paid. Hi tech always does something to produce low-tech jobs.

The high-pitched scream of a police car, followed by the howl of the siren of a fire engine interrupted my view into the future of the workplace. The noise evidently had a profound effect on the Guide, because he faded from my sight and then reappeared and then faded again. He was pulsing on and off as if in time with the sirens. As the Doppler effect took over, the Guide's appearances stayed a few seconds longer and his disappearances were a few seconds shorter. During the pulsing sensation, I couldn't understand what he was trying to impart to me. His thoughts as well faded in and out as if I was listening to a remote broadcast with fluctuating clarity. Finally the sirens were gone. A few seconds later a very dispirited-looking phantom remained, looking as solid as ever.

He held up his hand. "I don't want to talk about it. And that won't happen that often in the future, either."

Beginning in 2010, all new structures—private houses, schools, businesses, apartments, everything—in certain cities (and eventually everywhere) were constructed with virtual-reality firefighting equipment.

If a fire broke out in an office building, for example, a smoke, heat, and/or fire detector alerted the fire department. A remote firefighting technician at the fire department then swung into action. He didn't initiate any alarms or dispatch any trucks. He simply plugged into the building virtual-reality computer, and donned a helmet that looks like something out of *Star Wars*. With the helmet in place, he "found" himself inside the building. He could see all around him by just turning his head. In his hands were gloves that can sense heat and can deftly operate firefighting equipment such as water hoses. He can also sense other life forms such as people or animals—and even plants—and can determine if fire-smothering chemicals should be employed to put out the blaze. If he discovers life forms in harm's way, he can manipulate a number of pieces of apparatus that are stored in the walls of the buildings. Fireproof and heatproof tents can protect people and pets; clear bags can save plants or valuable artwork from chemicals. In 95 percent of all fires of the future, the fireman never puts on boots, coat, or hat. Much of the time, his work was to be so cut and dried that he won't even have to give up that hot supper he just sat down to when the alarm went off.

The first of these new-generation buildings will be constructed by 2010. Within fifteen years, all new construction—even garage sheds—will require the built-in anti-fire virtual-reality devices. By 2045, communities will begin retrofitting all dwellings and offices with the new systems—which will be constantly updated. After the year 2065, virtual-reality firefighting nearly eliminates all firemen. Firefighting vehicles will become as obsolete as the Linotype machine is for twentieth century newspapers.

"And we won't have to put up with those sirens," the Guide added with vehemence that seemed out of character for someone I had come to regard as a friendly spook.

The train rumbled uptown, screeching and rocking around curves in the track. The lights blinked off for seconds but the sparse Sunday group of riders reading their *New York Daily News* never missed a beat. The Guide hovered a few inches above his seat, avoiding some of the bumps and sways of the car. I was amused as I watched him misgauge the braking motion as we slid into Thirty-fourth Street. When the train stopped, he was sitting in the middle of a metal pole. "Done this often?" I chided him.

We walked up the steps of the station and into the sunny afternoon. He wanted to go look at Macy's and then we strolled leisurely across town and then up Fifth Avenue.

Virtual reality and the communications highway will redefine the way Americans shop for clothes, the Guide explained, but he said, "There will always be a certain fascination for people to go shop in the city, mingle with the crowds, and feel the excitement of a major city. New York will always be New York."

But shopping for a new dress will be another experience if you can't get to the city to do your shopping at Saks. A computer camera will take a three-dimensional portrait of you—all of you, all natural. "You'll just have to learn to trust the camera and the computer," the Guide said when I suggested that American women will not take their clothes off in front of a video camera for any reason. "And," he said, "the results will overcome any embarrassment."

The computer will store your figure in its virtual-reality compartment—updating it monthly or as necessary, depending on what you eat and how you exercise. Then you'll go shopping. You can dial up Macy's or Saks or Nieman-Marcus or Bullock's and program yourself a tour of the dress department. Using a virtual-reality connection and video cameras in the store, you can shop from rack to rack, checking out the clearance sales or the new items just in from the New York and Paris fashion runways. Virtual-reality sensors let you feel the material as if you were in the store yourself. The colors will be as true as if you were there, too.

Once you find a dress that suits your aesthetic eye as well as your pocketbook, you will actually try on the dress using your computer-stored figure. Naturally the computer will add undergarments so that you get a good representation of how the dress fits you. Then you can look at yourself wearing the dress. As you raise your arms or sit down or stroll along in your home you will see a portrait of yourself doing the same thing at the store. It will be like watching yourself in a movie or a television show.

Well, suppose it looks good to you. What about asking some experts to comment. With a flip of a button live consultants in fashion can take a brief glimpse of what you are wearing and comment on its practicality, tastefulness, fit, and how to accessorize the garment.

When you are fully satisfied with the purchase, and it has been computer-altered for a perfect fit by real-time tailors, you will pay for the clothes through an electronic transfer of funds between your bank and the store's bank. The garment will be expertly packaged—a whole new breed of packing technicians will be created by this application of virtual-reality technology—and dispatched to you by overnight delivery systems. You'll be able to shop for tomorrow night's gala today with confidence that what you'll be wearing will be up-to-date, flattering, and a perfect fit. For a premium, the store will be able to check its records and those of similar establishments to make sure that no one else going to the event will be wearing the same dress.

"Now, Shawn," he said, "for a guarantee like that wouldn't you be willing to undress?"

"No comment," I said. "Are men always so sure of themselves that they think that women will always be tied to fashion in this era or the next?"

"Some things never change, Shawn. Especially those factors about ourselves which are ingrained through history and environment. If they did change easily there would be no ghettos, no Bosnia, no prejudice. I would love to tell you that in the twenty-first century mankind has learned to overcome prejudice against the color of one's skin, sex, religion, or national origin or even regional origin. I can't tell you that. Many things change; many other things remain the same."

I turned away from the shop window displaying slinky dresses at Bonwit Teller's and turned to look across Fifth Avenue. "Watch your step," the Guide advised.

I glanced down at the sidewalk and froze as a pond of mud spread out in front of me. I tipped forward as my momentum carried me toward the mud, but I was able to grab onto a wooden fence that stopped my drop into the ooze.

In front of me a dozen of the largest hogs I had ever seen in my life—although I must admit that I'd never been that close to pigs of any size that hadn't already been reduced to filling a BLT.

I caught my breath and gave the Guide a withering look. "I'm waiting," I said, not at all calmly or in a forgiving tone.

"Tell your friends' kids who aren't going to be stockbrokers to grow up to be pig farmers. Trust me on this one," the Guide said.

In 2005, a thirty-seven-year-old cardiology researcher—who was dying of a genetic heart disorder—secretly injected a pig protein into the body of his newborn son. The researcher from the Mayo Clinic had been working for ten years—since his father died at the age of forty-two—on developing a vaccine that could save his own life. He realized by 2005 that he had succeeded—but it was too late for him.

The theory was that if he injected the pig protein in his newborn son, his son's body would develop a natural immunity to pig protein and if, as the researcher feared, the boy had the same genetic heart condition that had existed through five generations of the family that someday his boy was going to need a heart transplant.

The researcher had already received one donor heart, but this one was failing, too. He knew enough of the physiology involved to realize that there was no sense in giving him a third heart—it would be better off going to a person whose body wouldn't destroy it as his would.

By 2000, scientists had devised new, effective ways of preventing transplanted organs from being rejected by the host body. It worked like a charm in 95 percent of the cases—but there were major problems. There were those—such as the researcher—who still rejected the organs, and there weren't enough organs available to go around to the number of people who needed new hearts and other organs.

The researcher couldn't save himself, but he thought he might save his son. He injected his newborn son with the pig protein because he knew that only in newborns could the immune system learn to deal with pig protein. He knew that if his son developed the same disease he had—a foregone conclusion which proved to be accurate—then his son would need a new heart when he turned thirty in 2035. And the researcher knew that by the year 2035, tens of thousands of people in the United States and around the world would need transplants for their hearts—and there would not be nearly enough hearts to go around. The answer would have to be xenografts— taking the organ of one species and placing it in another species' body. The history of xenografts had been spectacular—spectacular failures. It was recognized after several attempts that the only successful way to make xenografts work was to vaccinate the potential donee with the protein of the donor species when the donee was born. The problem was: How could you convince the parents of newborns that they had to become part of an experiment which might be fatal, and which presumed that sometime in the future that baby was going to need a new organ—and there was no proof that the procedure would work? Scientists were stymied.

When the researcher died in 2008, he willed his scientific notebooks to a top cardiology research university in the Midwest, with the caveat that one volume of his work not be opened for ten years. In 2018, the university cracked open his notebooks and were horrified and intrigued by the experiment the researcher had performed. It was considered unethical for the researcher to have experimented on his own son. The researchers convinced the child's mother, now remarried and living in another state, to at least let them test the child to see if he had developed antibodies to pig protein as his father had predicted. Yes, the results proved that the antibodies were in the child's body, and, yes, they had found evidence that the boy also had the same genetic factors that made it likely he would need a heart transplant before he was thirty. The scientists concluded that because the child's body was familiar with pig protein, it might be possible to give him a xenograft.

The doctors now watching the youth grow up also knew that in the current era of transplant technology, a thirty-year-old candidate for a heart transplant would be rejected for surgery with another human heart. It would be a terrible waste of a valuable organ. The scientists realized that the boy's father knew what he was doing and they were galvanized into studying how to best put a pig's heart into this living experiment's body.

In 2033, the boy's heart began to fail. The first sign was a rapid heartbeat which had to be converted by medication. Doctors immediately implanted a combination pacemaker and defibrillator—to prevent abnormal heartbeats from reaching fibrillation and killing the young man in seconds—and drug pump. If the defibrillator was set off to control the arrhythmias, the pump would automatically disperse a few drops of antiarrhythmic drugs directly into the heart muscle. When the defibrillator began popping almost daily, the scientists knew it was time to see if the precedent-setting procedure really worked.

The operation in the spring of 2034 went smoothly. After fourteen days in the hospital—longer than most transplant cases who were now being sent home after two days—the man was discharged. He returned to the hospital once a week for six months while doctors tested his new heart for signs of rejection—a sign that meant death for the patient because doctors did not believe that even the newest antirejection drugs would work on a xenograft.

In 2035, the man was told that he only had to return to the hospital once every month; then every two months. He was still being tested regularly in 2037 when doctors declared the experiment a success and highly recommended that parents inoculate children at birth with pig protein so that twenty, forty, sixty years down the road they, too, could receive pig xenografts if something went wrong with the body.

Incredibly, only a year and a half after the first children were given the pig protein, one of the children was accidentally injured in a freak automobile accident. A gasoline truck explosion a mile and a half away spewed metal shrapnel into the air. A piece of the metal came down in the roof of the car where the baby was riding and a sliver of metal was driven through the girl's heart. Somehow the child was still alive—pinned to her baby seat by the mini metal javelin. Paramedics rushed her to the hospital where doctors realized that too much damage had been done. But the girl's mother, a nurse, knew she had been given pig protein. A right-sized pig heart was quickly located and was implanted in the girl in the emergency cardiac care unit. She survived and never showed any sign of rejection. Both she and the original pig heart recipient were still alive by the end of the twenty-first century.

In 2041, the researcher who had injected his son with the pig protein was awarded, posthumously, the Nobel Prize for medicine. And pig farming became one of the most lucrative businesses in the world.

6

HOME SEEKERS

"SO, WHAT DO YOU THINK?" THE GUIDE ASKED.

He pointed at the house, a two-story comfortable-looking building on a green patch of lawn, surrounded by other similar-styled structures.

"It looks okay to me," I said. "But what do I know about houses?" What I really wanted to know was: Where was I and how did I get here? I didn't even recall getting out of bed—am I asleep? Or is the Guide making one of his impromptu appearances? I searched my memory for some indication of how I'd gotten wherever it was that I was.

In the meantime, the Guide was quizzing me about home-buying.

"Ah, the point is," he said, "that all you see here is a house. Apparently well built and well maintained. But there is a lot more to the story. In the twenty-first century you aren't going to be able to assume that the house you buy is the place where you want to live. Remember the Love Canal story. The process of buying a home in the next century is going to mean that you need help in finding a decent location to live."

The Guide opened up a telephone book—I have no

idea how he conjured up the tome—and showed me the listings under "home consultants."

"This one, 'City Seekers,' is the oldest company which specializes in finding out everything there is to know about your prospective house," the Guide said.

Today, a lawyer orders a thorough title search to determine if there are any legal liens on the house or if the mortgage holder three generations ago was fully paid for the home. The title search makes sure that the house is really, legally yours. But the lawyer doesn't find out if the land is built over a cemetery or a landfill or is next door to a penitentiary.

"There were horror stories in the 1990s and early twenty-first century," the Guide explained. "One couple in New Jersey were literally scared out of their home by apparitions and odors and strange sounds that rattled through the home."

The couple was mystified by the eerie shrieks that seemed to erupt from the basement of their home. They immediately thought about ghosts and goblins but discarded those ideas because their lot was in a brand-new development. There were a couple of other occupied homes and a number of other houses under construction.

Although embarrassed by the noises and their fears, they finally traipsed across the open fields and around building materials and earthmovers to knock on the door of their nearest neighbors. What they found was interesting—their neighbors had also experienced strange phenomena. They also discovered that all four of the families now living in the development were from out of state. The families decided that something had to be done to investigate what was happening, but the local newspaper was uninterested in alleged ghostly activities; the Better Business Bureau was only concerned about construction flaws which, the home owners agreed, were no problem in the buildings themselves.

It took a few months of research, but finally the

families figured out what was going on: The development was built over a cemetery. A local priest who admitted outside the confines of the church that he was familiar with demons, ghosts, and exorcisms confirmed that the noises and apparitions were ghosts of the formerly interred. The construction company violated no laws and complied with all state laws regarding the renovation of the cemetery into building lots, so the families had no legal recourse. Closed-door meetings with lawyers and judges showed that no one would accept haunting as a reasonable reason for cancelling their contracts and mortgages on the homes. The developer told the new homeowners that if they wanted to he would buy back the homes on two conditions: The price would be less than what the homeowner paid, about 5 percent less—and the homeowners could never tell anyone why they left. Faced with a modest loss or a life shared with unwanted, angry ghosts, three of the four homeowners moved out. The fourth stayed put because they were a childless couple and the spooks that seemed to be inhabiting their house were childlike and relatively friendly for lost souls. The family also decided to stay because, in an era where construction ripoffs occurred daily, the contractors on this project were, at least, good at putting up a solid structure.

Others moved in because the shortage of affordable housing made the prospect of living with a ghost more reasonable than living with a mother-in-law.

But that incident led the former homeowners to go to home consultants to find their next house. Buying a home with a ghost is far preferable to buying a home built upon a "reclaimed" landfill.

I was aghast. "You can build homes on top of a cemetery? Aren't there laws against that? That's terrible." I thought of my grandfather's grave and wondered if someday there would be a duplex over his gravesite. Aren't graveyards forever? I wondered. Apparently not.

The Guide snorted. "Look what they've done to the

graveyards and sacred places of the natives of this land. They desecrate them and often they don't even know that the desecration is taking place," he said. And explained another task of the home consultant.

One of the nastiest problems of the twenty-first century occurred in Arizona in 2022. Land developers years before had managed to get approval to build a massive development near Sedona, considered by many people to be one of the psychic hot spots on earth. No one paid much attention to objections of local Native Americans who claimed that the area where the homesites was being placed were lying on top of sacred ritual lands. The bulldozers just moved in and were followed by masons, carpenters, roofers, and landscapers. Within a few months there were hundreds of people living in the development and thousands of Native Americans with, pardon the pun, ruffled feathers.

The natives tried to use the legal apparatus, but were unable to make justice work for their cause. They tried to negotiate with the builders and then the homeowners' association but they were rebuffed at every turn. Radicals among the native groups demanded action, and meanwhile more and more houses sold and more and more retirees, psychic groupies or wannabees, and young homeowners moved into the relatively inexpensive homes.

Then one chilly fall night in 2022, more than 100 Native Americans on horseback rode through Sedona Flats Estates and threw burning torches into living room windows and onto the wood shingle roofs of the homes in the estate. Some homeowners who were awakened by the pounding hooves of the horses were able to put out the flames and some with guns were able to shoot some of the intruders. More than two hundred houses were set ablaze in the awful night, and 128 of the homes were destroyed. Remarkably, loss of life was light: Ten residents died; seven of the midnight riders perished either through bullets or accident, including one Native American beaten to death when he stopped to rescue a small child and his parents from a flaming home.

The homes were insured, but insurance companies declined to reinsure the homes. The Native Americans held out the threat of additional attacks and attempts by law enforcement officials to track down the assailants proved to be futile. Slowly but surely, the Sedona Flats Estates became a modern ghost town. Native American agencies hastened the demise of the community by using monies earned from reservation casinos to buy out the homeowners who remained.

The Sedona Incident, as it became known, inspired other Native Americans to quietly but effectively force other settlers to move away from sacred grounds. One of the more effective strategies to accomplish the peaceful movement was for dozens—or as many as possible, in some cases hundreds—of Native Americans to appear in full regalia on horseback and surround a new home or homesite under construction. They would simply stand stoically still around the house. One member of the group would approach on foot, walking his horse behind him, and hand the homeowner a paper that listed the objections to building a home in that particular place. Usually the show of force was enough for the homeowner to seek another place to live. There was however a cost that the homeowner paid in giving up his land. Rarely could he collect to recover his expenses; rarely could he sell the land—although often the Native Americans were able to find some funds to salve the monetary loss.

It became imperative for the home consultant to warn prospective home buyers of such problems. In fact, in 2033, one homeowner successfully sued a home consultant for malpractice because the homeowner was not warned that the wonderful hill on his property was a sacred burial mound of a midwestern tribe. The tribe was quite vigorous in convincing the new owners to abandon their property. The homeowner got his money back by taking the consultant to court.

Despite this setback for the industry, the United States population in the twenty-first century was remarkably mobile. And conversely it made the home consultant job one of the most secure professions in the twenty-first century. It was a job that almost demanded an encyclopedic knowledge of one's community, so not only was employment secure in the field, it was also a position that didn't require anyone to move around a lot in order to move ahead. It wasn't an easy job, either. People wanted to know if the house they were going to buy with their nest egg was not only well-constructed but was worth living in.

Early in the twenty-first century one municipal or private landfill after another was closed because of increasing government regulation or simply because the landfill no longer had any room for trash. The filled-up fills were covered with dirt, replanted, and turned back over to municipalities. After a decade of lying unused—some became parks—many of the landfills were auctioned by municipalities to private developers. The developers were particularly interested in the landfills in Florida and other sunbelt communities. In some cases the landfills became amusement parks, or industrial and business developments or housing developments.

The Florida boom of the 1970s, 1980s, and 1990s slowed in the first fifteen years of the twenty-first century, mainly because there wasn't enough land in the desirable locations in South Florida. There was plenty of land in Central Florida and not far inland along the northern Atlantic Coast, and there were acres and acres available in the Florida Panhandle. But if you were leaving New York, Philadelphia, Boston, or Hartford for sunny Florida you didn't want to freeze in the months of December, January, and February. And in northern Florida and the Panhandle, freezing to death in those months was a real possibility.

The Guide said in aside, "Remember the headline in the *Daily News* last Thanksgiving when the temperature dropped to thirty-one in Pensacola: 'Florida shivers in freezing weather.' Sure, Pensacola. It didn't mention that in Fort Lauderdale it was eighty-two. South Florida. That's where the sunworshippers go to play or retire."

But in South Florida there was no land available until the developers started buying up closed landfills. In addition to being able to purchase the landfills from municipalities for far less than land would have cost if the land were available, the landfills offered something that natural South Florida didn't have—a view. The landfills were among the highest places in all of South Florida. Five miles from the ocean, developers could promise homebuyers a view of the Atlantic from their front windows. Migrating homeowners were taken in by Hillside Acres, Atlantic Terrace, Everglades Lookout Estates, and dozens of other wonderful-sounding places lined with trees (trucked in from nurseries which did a land office business in making the landfills more scenic), curving mountain-like roads (which followed the routes thousands of dump trucks has followed in previous years), and with prestigious addresses in Martin, Palm Beach, and Broward counties.

For homeowners who moved into these developments there was always a faint odor of decay that seemed to seep into the home; occasionally methane gas failed to leave through normal vents and worked its way into a home—exploding in flame and destroying the house and everything in it. Other times, these methane gases created their own vents, and suddenly a homeowner found out that he had a permanent geyser of flame in his backyard.

So the home consultants tried to locate where the landfills were located—even if you didn't buy on a former landfill, having one a hundred yards up the road could make for some strange whiffs when the wind direction changed.

But building on or near or even in a landfill or a cemetery isn't the only bad thing that can happen and did happen to people who thought that buying a home was simple enough that you didn't have to call in a consultant.

Take the case of a couple in Connecticut who found a plot of land overlooking a beautiful wooded glen. They were assured by the seller that the land in the glen was owned by the state and there were no plans to ever develop the property. They set about to build their dream house overlooking the land, sinking their life savings into the project. A year after having constructed the home, they were awakened in the middle of the night to discover half a dozen armed men in their home. They were tied up, gagged, and left sitting in their nightclothes in the middle of their living room when they were liberated the next day by state police.

On the other side of the glen, they were now informed, beyond the tree line, was one of the state's maximum-but-not-so-secure jails. They were captured by six of the most brutal criminals in the state—police were simply amazed that they hadn't been slaughtered. In fact, the escapees only took clothes, money, raided the refrigerator, and stole their car.

After a week with relatives, the couple returned to their home and now began exploring the beautiful glen. It was crisscrossed with trails under the tree canopies, many of which went directly to the other side of the glen. Once over the top of the glen, all they had to do was walk a couple of hundred yards to see the fifteen-foot-tall chain-link fences topped with razor wire and also see the guard houses mounted atop the brick prison walls inside the fences. Overall, it was a quick fifteen-minute trot from the prison walls to their home. They moved not long after the incident, selling to another couple who didn't use a home consultant.

While it's relatively simple to find out if you are living next door to a maximum security jail, the job of the home consultant was to find out if there was a juvenile crime halfway house down the street; or if that modern-looking high school doubled as a shock camp for borderline juvenile criminals.

The national home consultants worked with the local groups because only people living in the neighborhoods could tell you if the storefront on the corner was a place where itinerant day job workers went to find menial road camp jobs. Often, if there weren't enough jobs for the ditch-digging or lawn-cutting details, those that didn't get a job roamed the neighborhoods looking for jobs on their own—or anything they could steal, rape, or set afire.

The job of the home consultant was never done: The consultant's job was to make your home safe from human or naturally occurring hazards. The consultants checked for landfills, cemeteries, nearness to prisons, work camps, and penitentiaries; whether there had been a major earthquake in the last twenty years; locations of major power lines; paths of frequent hurricanes; the likelihood of floods, uncontrolled brush fires, or landslides; the location of mineral mining and slag heaps that could leech chemicals into ground water. The areas were checked for cancer deaths which marked some areas as lethal and others as safe; the location of nuclear reactors; the location of publicly identified hazardous-waste sites and privately cited waste cites that didn't make national lists; the crime rates of the state, county, city, and district where the home was being considered.

And the home consultant also had to determine cost of living, cost of housing, common patterns of local discrimination, general climate, nearness to educational, shopping, governmental, and recreational facilities.

Particularly worrisome to the homeowner was the potential for setting up a happy home on top of or close to a hazardous-waste dump. One couple in Salt Lake City claimed that their child, a certified genius, was really a mutant—certainly the virtual lack of any intellectual properties of the parents lent credibility to their claim—who obtained his enhanced brain power by the fact that a stream that flowed through their property was downstream from one of the many hazardous-waste sites in the United States. That family was the exception. Instead there was one heartbreaking story after another of children born with cleft palates, missing arms or legs or eyes or brains; women who found that after a year of living in a certain area they were unable to maintain normal menstrual cycles or suffered one miscarriage after another; men whose sperm count dropped to almost nothing; young children who came down with bizarre and incredible rare cancers or skin lesions.

The home seekers tried to find not only the 1,200 government registered superfund waste dump sites to clean up (by 2061, only 250 of the sites had been cleaned up and the land made habitable—according to government allowances—again). The consultants also hunted down the locations for more than thirty thousand other hazardous-waste dump sites which weren't considered bad enough to be included on the superfund list. Of course, living next to any of these "not so bad" sites was dangerous to the health of every man, woman, child, and domestic pet that lived there. Most of the native wildlife either figured out that it wasn't safe to live there or hadn't figured it out and died miserably.

7

HEALTH ISSUES

I WAS PROFOUNDLY AFFECTED NOT ONLY BY MY VIS-
itation of this unknown entity from another dimension in time—but also the spectacular visions of the
future before me, especially, the mating of computers,
microengineering, and health, which will produce one of
the most magnificent breakthroughs in science as early
as 2017.

Scientists will create multifaceted, powerful computers
that are smaller than human cells. These micro-
biocomputers, complete with devices that can sense
changes in cells and have the ability to communicate
with other similar devices in the body as well as to
communicate through telemetry to doctors in their clin-
ics, will be contained in a fluid—a low-viscosity liquid
of myriad computer chips—that will be used to vaccinate people.

The computers will actually grow with the body. Constructed of inert materials, the microscopic devices will
be powered by the chemicals already present in the
body. But the amount of chemicals needed to power
these tiny machines will be the equivalent of eating one
extra carrot a year.

After a long series of experiments in animals, the first use of the computer vaccine in human beings will begin in the United States in 2011. The computers will be injected into middle-aged, healthy volunteers who have a family predisposition to cancer. The computers will affix themselves to certain receptor ports on cells of the major organs and will collect data on the body. Every six months, the volunteer patient will report to a doctor's office where a hand-held telemetry device will retrieve the accumulated data from the computers.

The results will be astounding. Not only will the devices work like a charm in every person—without regard to sex or body weight or body fat—but doctors will be able to pinpoint very early changes in cells that herald the onset of cancer. With the computers showing where the deadly cells are located, laser surgeons will thread fiber-optic devices into blood vessels and even into organs to locate the offending cells and vaporize them.

The quantum leap that the experiments give researchers allow for further developments. The next generation of experiments, beginning in 2014, will allow the various computers in the body to communicate among themselves. The first applications of this internal discussion of computers will be in athletes and models and the clinically obese. Before being injected with the computers, the volunteers will have desired weight and muscle-mass codes written into the computers that will be targeted to reside in muscles and the brain.

If too much fat begins to be deposited in the muscles, a signal will be sent to the brain computer which will initiate action to speed up metabolism internally, allowing for the unwanted fat to be burned off. Side effects of this procedure—a low-grade fever, gastrointestinal upset, unusual and intense perspiration rates—will be deemed acceptable for people whose lives and livelihoods demand that the body maintain a certain weight and form. Scientists will secretly breathe a collective sigh of relief that the side effects are uncomfortable enough to keep the average person from using the computer techniques as a diet aid.

By 2017, with almost daily improvements and successes being recorded in the bio-computer field, the government will pay for mass inoculations of newborns with the micro-computers. While the decision to enter a child into the massive experiment will be considered "voluntary," regulators will succeed in almost 100 percent acceptance by ruling that children who are not vaccinated by the computers will be ineligible for federal health insurance programs.

As would be expected by such a pronouncement, certain religious and civil rights organizations will protest, declaring that it is the right of parents to choose if their children shall be given the vaccinations. Since the procedure is still considered an experiment, the courts will allow those who wish to avoid the vaccination to do so without losing insurance. By 2030, however, the success of the system will remove any doubt about the vaccination's ability to keep people healthy. Children will be required to have the vaccination just as certain as birth blood tests have been required for decades. Religious objections will continue to be allowed by the courts, but even most of the extreme religious groups will recognize the remarkable ability of the vaccination process to keep people alive and well and by 2050 universal vaccination will be virtually accomplished.

Here's how the system will work:

The microscopic computers will be injected into the bloodstream of infants at birth. The computers will be targeted to reach certain organs of the body. Some computers will be attracted by monoclonal antibodies to settle in the liver; others will monitor the pancreas, the heart, the brain, the lungs.

If an abnormality appears, the computer will have three missions: Collect data on the manifestation, send for help, and send a warning to the host. The microchip, for example, in the coronary arteries that provide blood to the heart, would be able to sense the growth of plaque inside the artery. The need to attack this plaque build-up isn't necessary until more than 60 percent of the artery wall is blocked. When that happens the computer on the wall of the artery will signal a computer elsewhere in the bloodstream, calling for specialized cells to attack the blockage on the artery, and dissolve it.

However, because such buildups are known to develop in people who are predisposed to such formations in the arteries, the computer will send a message to another computer located in the palms of the person's hands. That computer will cause a rash to appear on the palm, a rash that will form as a recognizable symbol to the patient. Upon seeing the symbol, the patient will call his physician, who can get a telemetry readout of the computers simply by having the patient place the telephone receiver at various places on his body. Patients will recognize the rash because it will appear every six months as a reminder to have a checkup by his doctor. The doctor will be able to hit a button on a telephone to inform the computer that it has received the information and the computer will turn off the bio-mechanism which causes the rash.

The computers will be successful in telling doctors who is at risk of disease, and will be able to raise the alarm that the disease is developing, and even will be able to coordinate an attack on the disease process within the body. But for many people, this isn't going to be enough. That's why communication with the doctor will be necessary because surgical repair of blood vessel ruptures or the need for medications to control the disease process will still be necessary.

The bio-computers will be hailed as the medical breakthrough of the millennium in developed countries, but in areas of Asia, Africa, and South America that were devastated by the ongoing AIDS catastrophe, the computers will be regarded with suspicion and fear.

The decision to vaccinate the third-world's children with the bio-computers is greeted by controversy everywhere. In the developed world, health care economists argue that to provide the vaccinations is expensive and worthless because the developing countries do not have the sophisticated telecommunications and medical facilities to make use of the system. "What good is it to be able to allow doctors to examine a body over the telephone—if the people don't have access to a telephone?" critics will charge. Others will note that even if the diseases are detected through improved telecommunication links, the technology to correct defects is not available universally.

But the proponents of the plan will counter that to not vaccinate now and to wait for everything to be in place will delay the best of health care for another half a century. "Vaccinate now," they say, "and by the time diseases first appear, twenty to forty years later, the health care implements will be in place."

After years of wrangling, the World Health Organization will finally get approval to proceed with universal vaccination. The first area to get the vaccinations will be Central Africa in 2033.

When that attempt to vaccinate the children begins, the first of the Red Cross Massacres occurs. Militants in the Central African Republic, squeezed by the presence of United Nations troops and the unrelenting death from AIDS, begin citing a long-discredited theory that AIDS was spread across Africa by the World Health Organization's 1970s campaign to eliminate smallpox.

The WHO was successful in removing the smallpox scourge from the face of the earth, but pseudoscientists and medical historians point to the coincidences between smallpox vaccinations and massive AIDS outbreaks in the Horn of Africa. Considerable detective work proves that the coincidences are just coincidences, that the cure of one disease did not create another deadlier problem. But the rumor and the hint of truth is embedded in the consciousness of the dying millions in Africa.

Led by frenzied mobs, the first group of Red Cross officials who attempt to vaccinate newborns at a hospital in Bangui, the capital of Central Africa, are brutally slain in the street outside the hospital. Nurses and doctors are hacked to death and are literally dismembered by the mob who hurl the body parts of the health workers at unprepared UN troops, who are caught flatfooted by the response to the vaccination attempts.

Word of the massacre spreads rapidly since every community in the world now has direct access to multilanguage CNN broadcasts. Team after team of Red Cross vaccinators are attacked and slaughtered. The only solution is to protect the doctors and nurses with troops and force the "voluntary" vaccination procedure. Instead of this draconian measure, the scientists give up their attempts to provide the bio-computers to the entire world.

8

MALL INCIDENT

THE PANIC ATTACK CAME ON SUDDENLY AND SWIFTLY.

I didn't have any warning to prepare myself for the events that followed next. One moment I was joyous and happy—and in the next breath I was gasping for air, feeling the constrictions in my chest as I tried to take in oxygen. I felt light-headed and dizzy, on the verge of passing out.

Just as suddenly as the panic attack came over me, it mysteriously disappeared, leaving me pale and shaken. But in that one split second before I felt my world coming apart, I saw before my eyes bloodshed and destruction, mutilated and burned bodies lying across a cold floor. I had to ask the Guide what this vision meant.

I didn't think it was possible for an apparition to look uncomfortable. But the Guide was clearly bothered by what I was asking.

"What you want to know is truly unimportant. There are many, many more important things you must learn," he said. "My time here is limited. The time you have to see me will not continue forever. There are others who must be contacted."

I sensed a threat. I felt that I was being toyed with

and a flash of playing poker with one of my uncles swept across my mind. He's bluffing, I thought. And I thought I saw an apparition blink.

"Look," I said, "most of the events and stories of the future would have been lost without you. I know that you are necessary for me to see what you want me to see and I know how important it is for me to understand what I've been shown. But this picture brings such torment to me that I must be able to explain it. I must be able to warn people about it."

He shook his head sadly. "Why must you bother with such trivia? Perhaps you are seeing an accident. So if it is an accident what could the casualties be—a score, a hundred, a thousand? Insignificance. If I take the time to show you this incident, I may not have time to explain how the deaths of millions can be avoided in a war.

"Accidents will always occur. They are tragedies but they do not destroy civilizations. Accidents cause sadness but we can't predict accidents; they are a part of life as is everything else. Your warning will not save the lives of these people you see in the dream. But you can save countless others."

In the wave of messages sent to me at Auriesville, one particular sequence haunted me and kept me from sleep. In a dreamlike horror, I could see mothers and children being consumed by unremitting walls of flame. I was alternately chilled to the bone and then burned by the conflagration I was witnessing. I could make out buildings and the time—the year 2003—but everything else was a blur.

"I may not be able to save everyone's life," I cried to the Guide, "but I can see these people dying in front of me and if I can see that they are dying then there must be something I can do to save them."

In my mind I could see these poor victims and I instantly recalled the horror in the eyes of those poor doomed people on that DC-10 so many years before.

No, I hadn't saved them. But I had tried. Damn, I would try again.

Again I confronted the Guide. "I can't believe that these people I see are so unimportant if my vision is so clear.

"You must tell me what this means. I won't go on with the other visions until you help me see this one clearly," I told him. I was bluffing, of course, but I hoped he didn't know that. The Guide's comments about his limited time with me were real, I knew. Several times I wanted to ask about more details and I found he was difficult to reach. He didn't answer my thoughts or my voice. I'd seen him fade before my eyes and just vanish as the apparition he was.

He took my hand. "Do you like the cold?" he asked abruptly.

The mall appeared beside me. I jumped aside as a child about three years of age raced past me. A frantic adult, loaded down with several brightly-colored packages, lurched after him. The boy darted in and out of the crowded corridors of the mall. The sounds of people walking and talking, the jingle of a Salvation Army Santa encouraging donations filled the air. Above the cacophony, I could distinctly hear the sound of a calliope and the squeals of little children.

Instantly I was aware of the location, the giant mall at the north end of Syracuse, New York. I'd seen the mall before as I traveled through the state. It was a massive enterprise with scores of shops from the pricey to the bargain basement. I turned to the Guide, but he too had vanished into the crowds. I looked around the multitiered shopping center. A row of flickering lights spelled out the drama: two more days till Christmas.

The clock on the wall read 4:45 PM. I was lured outside, and now I understood the Guide's words. The freezing air chills me in seconds. My eyes winced as huge snowflakes slapped against my face and stung my cheeks. I couldn't believe what I was seeing. There was a near blizzard—nothing new for Syracuse—but the mall was jammed; the parking lots were filled to capacity and a parade of cars followed each other through row after row of cars, searching desperately for parking spaces that didn't exist.

I felt myself being turned towards the west (the Guide?), I thought. Through the stormy skies I could see across the mall parking lot to the round, flat structures just across the street. It took a few seconds before I realized that the fifty-foot-high buildings were the structures I'd seen in the vision. Recognition swept across me: I realized that I knew what those structures were. The words finally came to me: a tank farm.

The cold bit through me, but it had nothing to do with the weather. I shivered as I recounted in my mind the screams and the anguish of the people around me. "Go home. Get out of here," I began yelling at the people hustling to get out of the snowy frenzy of cars and shoppers and snowflakes. But no one could hear me.

The noise startled me. *Pock-a-ta, pock-a-ta, pock-a-ta.* The television helicopter's vortex raised funnel clouds of snow as the crew prepared for a live shot of the shopping finale for the local news. The helicopter slowly circled the mall, rising up and down with gusts and drafts.

Horror started to close in on me as the vision and reality began to merge. From the east, I could see another helicopter, a rival station, approach to film the same shot—a natural for two days before Christmas in 2003. I watched as my dream came true. The second helicopter moved in for a closer shot, hovering at a higher altitude than the first camera crew. A gust of wind blew a powerful wall of snow off Onondaga Lake and across the mall, obscuring the mall from the vision of the cameramen on both helicopters.

One helicopter moved up and to the east; the other tried a lower altitude. A sudden lull in the wind created an aerodynamic vacuum and the flying machines veered towards each other as if sucked into a giant vacuum. The main rotor of one of the helicopters clipped the rear rotor of the other, severing it and sending the spinning blade across the road and through the side of the gasoline-laden tanks, about twenty-two feet off the ground.

The spurting gasoline arched out of the tank and splashed on the roadway, creating a river of golden liquid that followed the ruts in the snow downhill to the entrance of the mall.

Its tail rotor gone, the fatally stricken helicopter spiraled helplessly towards the ground. The other helicopter, missing two feet of main rotor, wobbled unhealthily in the sky, trying to find purchase on the buffeting winds.

The first copter rolled on its side and then dropped like a stone into a row of cars still looking for a place to park. For an instant nothing more happened. Then a sheet of flame arose from the crumpled craft and an explosion tore what was left of the copter into burning fragments. The concussion shattered the windows of the mall, and literally knocked shoppers on the upper floors of the mall over the railings and into the abyss between the stores.

Flaming wreckage leaped all over the building and one spark found the lake of gasoline curling around the outside of the mall structure. As if in slow motion a wall of flame climbed from the street, engulfing pedestrians, cars, and the mall itself. Rapidly the flames raced backward to the road and then unthinkingly climbed the spurting gasoline waterfall like a salmon swimming upstream and reached the site of the leak.

Again there was a pause, but it was brief. The tank spurting the gasoline was literally there one second and gone the next, consumed by a fireball that was seen twenty-five miles away. Among the first victims of the blast were the crew of the second helicopter, just one hundred yards away when the fireball surrounded the craft and disintegrated it in the air.

The destruction wasn't over. One by one, other tanks

in the farm failed in the intense heat, adding more fuel and greater explosions to the scene of the catastrophe. Rescue teams couldn't get near the site due to the danger of explosions which seared the evening sky every five to ten minutes. These gigantic blasts rattled windows and hurled debris miles—one piece of metal tore a monstrous hole into the fabric roof of the Syracuse University Carrier Dome five miles away.

If this wasn't enough, these huge blasts were accompanied by small yet significant explosions as one car after another exploded in the flames and debris-littered parking lot of the mall.

Those few lucky survivors in the west end of the building and the parking lot ran mindlessly away from the hell their holiday had become. Some people were crushed by others as the mall burst into flames that quickly devoured the merchandise-packed stores. Others were killed when they ran on the expressway north of the mall in an attempt to escape the catastrophe.

The death toll reached thousands, with as many serious injuries.

I stood in the midst of the ruins. I was crying as flames rose around me. "Now you know," the Guide said. "It was just an accident. Perhaps an accident of epic proportions, but these things happen. We can't change all the disasters that man and technology create for themselves. There is risk in living. We can't control that and neither can you. If you tell people about this perhaps they will do something. Maybe they will heed the warnings about eliminating the tank farms or relocating the facility. Maybe they'll ban helicopters from flying over the mall. Maybe they'll just laugh at you and pay no attention. Maybe they'll do everything that should be done and the disaster will still occur."

I reminded the Guide of his oath to me. "You said you would never lie or mislead me. Yet aren't you saying just that: That what I am seeing or what I am feeling isn't true."

The Guide replied, "This is the Truth as it is today. You humans, you living people are not our puppets. You can make choices. If the choices we predict from what we know about humans which we have learned over millennia do not occur when we say they will occur it is because someone did something to change the events.

"There is an old adage that claims that if a butterfly flaps its wings in China, it will rain in Miami—or something like that. Your job is to provide the warning. It's up to others to hear the siren and then to heed its alarm.

"You can't make them do that. I can't make them do that. All we can do is wait, hope, and pray."

He kicked at a gnarled windshield wiper in the mounds of soot amid the gently falling snow. "This was sacred land to the Onondaga five hundred years ago. These," he said, spreading his arms wide and turning in a circle, "were the lands of my forefathers; lands the gods gave to us to raise our families and hunt our game and raise our crops. We once were proud to walk here, but today we walk on fields that are filled only with agony and a curse that will live for centuries."

He looked around. I could see that the apparition could feel anguish and could understand sadness.

"I had to know," I said.

He nodded. "By the way," he smiled grimly, "I knew you were bluffing."

9

THE MIDDLE EAST

THE SCENE ALONG THE BEACH WAS IMPRESSIVE AS THE guide and I strolled unseen across the warm white sands and gazed into the unrelenting sun out over the azure waves lapping gently at the shore.

The Guide pointed inland, and a forest of condominiums caressed the dunes, and behind the condos and hotels, one could make out the bright lights of casinos and gaming houses, themselves dwarfed by giant skyscrapers, emblazoning the names of the world's largest banks in various languages.

Along the crowded beach men, women, and children frolic in the sand and water, wearing assorted bathing suits—or no attire at all.

"The fruits of peace," the Guide says, admiring a coven of women clad only in the tiniest of thongs, "are wealth, beauty, and the pursuit of happiness."

As I view the scene about me and watch as people pass alongside us, never even glancing at my Guide, dressed in his Native American garb and myself in my nightgown, I'm puzzled. Where are we? I think to myself.

The Guide answers, "Gaza. You are in Gaza, the showplace of the Mediterranean. The Jewel of Friendship. The proof that even in the twenty-first century there can be success. That light and hope and trust can result in something worthwhile."

The words I had written months before, the scenes of streets and, what I thought of as fanciful, Arabs and Jews walking arm-in-arm down a street, now began to make sense. The Guide took me to a bench looking out over the blue Mediterranean Sea. We sat, and the story of peace unfolded in my mind.

The agreement by Israel and the Palestine Liberation Organization to recognize each other in 1993 put an end to generations of bloodshed and resentment between the two warring factions. It didn't end the killing and strife. Too much blood had been spilled; too many atrocities by both sides over the decades hardened the hearts of millions of Israelis and Palestinians. There were still terrorist bombings of buses and schools; crazed individuals slaughtered others out of mindless hatred and hopeless attempts to stem the tide of peace.

But while the road to war is often a helpless descent to Hell, the road to peace builds momentum slowly. The sheer mass of numbers of people and hopes of centuries cannot slow down the desire to live in harmony. Once the carrot of peace is made available, a few individuals cannot stop that progress.

Without official backing of the Israeli government, the hard-line Jewish settlers and extra-governmental organizations could not maintain their positions. The slowly developing Palestinian government rejected violence and rejected those who advocated violence. Without official backing neither the Israelis or Palestinians who opposed peace could long endure. Violence became less frequent, then random, and then descended into simple criminal activity.

By the year 2006, peace was firmly entrenched in the Holy Land, and the biggest winner of all was Palestine. The agreements to give autonomy to Gaza and the West Bank territories, of course, took far longer than first suggested. Five years stretched into ten, and ten to fifteen. But by 2018, no one really cared that Palestine was still not independent because it really was independent.

The best thing that happened to Palestine and especially Gaza was the Israeli insistence that Israel would always provide security—i.e., the army—to "protect" Palestine. In practice, however, Egypt agreed—actually begged—to protect southern Gaza where it borders Egypt; Israel provided the tight security along Gaza's borders with Israel; on the West Bank crack Jordanian troops patrolled the Jordan River border with the West Bank of Palestine; and Israeli troops watched the rest of the borders with Israel.

When the original multinational agreements were signed, the Palestinians were concerned that without their ability to protect themselves they could never call themselves truly independent. But after a number of years, the Palestinians realized that outside protection was the best thing that could have ever happened to them. Palestine was now free of the immense financial burden of a national defense. The entire tax and revenues of the state could be spent on social services and the building of a national infrastructure.

Schools were built, gleaming highways were constructed, universities sprang up overnight along with hospitals, municipal buildings, gigantic malls, and placid, luxuriant mosques. There was a building frenzy.

The international protection also gave the fledgling state something that no other nation in the Middle East could guarantee—safety for its citizens from outside attack, and a safe haven for business.

Arab governments which for decades had sent funds to Switzerland or Liechtenstein or invested in London and New York now saw it as their duty to fellow Arabs and fellow Muslims and their desire to improve their personal wealth to invest in Palestine—and specifically to invest in Gaza.

"Why not in Jericho or in the West Bank?" I asked the Guide.

"In fact," he said, "there is considerable investment in the West Bank. Millions of dollars and millions of gold rials have been spent in archaeological digs sponsored by some of the major universities in Arab countries to excavate historical sites on the West Bank. Major museums and tourist attractions are established across that area which makes it a tourist mecca.

"But if you are going to visit your money, do you want to visit it among farmland and small villages or would you rather lounge by the sea or go visit one of the many gaming houses that made the province of Gaza the 'A' ticket for travel?

"Additionally, there is a continuing problem with religious fundamentalism. On the West Bank, with so many historical sites that are sacred to Judaism, Christianity, and the Muslim world, the idea of a casino, dancing girls, and nude sunbathers was put to death quickly by a much more conservative, religious populace."

The West Bank development was led by the location of the seat of national government in Jericho and, by fiat, in Jerusalem; the nation's farming industry and its major schools and colleges are also located on the West Bank. Gaza, essentially, had nothing at the time that peace took hold. It did have one major exploitable natural resource—its shoreline. And with military stability ensured, the resort entrepreneurs moved in and began building seaside hotels and restaurants. Highways and high-speed rail lines linking Tel Aviv and Cairo were quickly constructed. A huge international supersonic jetport, constructed in a joint Israeli-Egyptian-Palestinian venture and financed by Saudi Arabia and the Gulf emirates, was built in the desert straddling the international boundary between Egypt and Israel—a huge white line painted across the runway, and even the terminal building reminded visitors that while there is international cooperation there remain national sovereignty issues.

With all this construction and the tens of thousands of jobs created, unemployment virtually disappeared for the Palestinians. The money being dumped into Palestine to build the country created the need for banks. Workers needed a place to cash paychecks and to build savings. Workers who succeeded with savings needed loans to build housing and buy new cars and trucks.

And all work and no play makes workers of every faith and race dull, so the prosperity abloom required the development of diversions. The casinos sprung up quickly and by 2010, Gaza was the destination of people from around the world. The jetport—which was built with enough forethought to allow Gaza International to be one of the ten landing sites for the Space Plane— meant that within the time it usually took to go from Chicago to New York, a traveler could fly from almost anywhere in the world to the gambling tables and ocean breezes of Gaza.

The success of Gaza and the West Bank rendered all other problems between Israel and its Arab neighbors as meaningless. The fifty-year-long boycott of firms doing business with Israel was ended. Informal cracks appeared in the boycott before the end of the century and by the time the boycott was officially put to death at the start of the new millennium, its effectiveness was nonexistent.

The ability to live in peace and harmony extended outside of the region to areas where peace wasn't considered an option. The greatest success of the need for peace, outside of Palestine and Israel, was in Lebanon where one of the major rebuilding efforts in one hundred years resulted in the rebuilding of Beirut.

The thorniest question of all—the status of Jerusalem—was solved in the most unique way of all. Neither Israel nor Palestine did anything about it. So great was the cooperation of former warring parties that the solution to Jerusalem came about without the input or conflict between either party.

In 2012, with Gaza already booming and the number of incidents along the borders of Israel and Palestine being reduced to finding smugglers of archaeological artifacts, the government of Saudi Arabia proposed that it finance the protection of religious sites sacred to Islam throughout the world. Ostensibly, the offer was made after a small riot in April of that year occurred when a deranged pilgrim attempted to hurl paint on the Dome of the Rock. The riot occurred when Muslims attempted to beat the man to death and Israeli soldiers and policemen had to hammer a few bodies with nightsticks in order to rescue the defiler—a Muslim, by chance, who had deciphered phrases in the Koran which he interpreted to mean that major sacred structures had to be destroyed—of the sacred temple.

While that meant that certain temples in places such as Bangladesh and Timbuktu would benefit by having highly trained police guard sites to protect them against such actions, the real point was to extinguish another hot spot in Arab-Israeli relations. For now, so much enterprise existed between the nations of the Middle East that no side dared endanger the relationship.

The Israelis reluctantly agreed to the plan, recognizing that the country was giving up a piece of its own sovereignty. But, as one member of the Israeli Knesset said, "When the price of peace is so small, only fools disdain it."

One of the places of religious and historical buildings which is guarded by the Saudi-financed troops is a relatively insignificant mosque which was built in 2004 and became more of a meeting hall for East Jerusalem Palestinians rather than strictly a place of worship. Now the Palestinian parliament which has been meeting since 1994 in Jericho moves its sessions to this building in Jerusalem.

There is outrage among Israelis who have been steadfast in refusing to give up any portion of the city to the Palestinians who also claim the city as its territory. But in a compromise that can especially be appreciated by both Jews and Arabs who have survived by bending with winds of change rather than allowing a hurricane to blow them away, the Palestinians give up their claims on Jerusalem as long as their parliament can meet there. The center of government for Palestine remains at Jericho where all the government agencies are located and where virtually all the government workers live. The decisions are simply made in Jerusalem.

In effect, the Palestinians renounce their claims to Jerusalem provided the decisions of their government can be made in the Holy City. The Israelis maintain their claims to the city, yet allow a foreign government to act as if Israeli territory is the foreigners' capital.

The understanding between Palestine and Israel works out well and by 2035, only a few dissidents in Palestine still clamor about the fact that Palestine is still not independent, and very few Israelis remain who protest that Palestine has taken over part of Jerusalem. The growth of Palestine and the stability among all states in the area by this time has even resulted in the elimination of border guards between keys points in Jerusalem. Traffic and commerce flow freely from Jerusalem to Jericho and Palestinian currency and postage stamps are accepted for use throughout Israel.

In Gaza, the northern border between Gaza and Israel has virtually disappeared as enterprising Israelis extend the line of condominiums and hotels north along the coast. Peace and prosperity reign over the Holy Land.

The Guide looks towards me, having laid out a landscape of peace that would be the highest hope of anyone who once despaired of ever finding peace in that troubled neighborhood.

But there is something strange about his face. It is a vision of terrible sadness. "You are grieving," I tell him, "yet you should be joyous."

He nods slightly, his lips tight. "Ah, but if only this was the entire story of how old strife can be overcome. If only this was the answer for all enemies on earth to resolve their differences. Not far from here the scene is very different."

He turns away from the sparkling beaches and the bikini-clad men and women frolicking on the hot sands of the white beaches and the azure blue waters of the Mediterranean.

I follow him with my eyes and turn my head to follow him—and I look into a field of horror. On the horizon, rushing with the force of a monstrous freight train, comes a wall of fire. A horrendous shock uproots the trees and flattens the grass around us and then a wave of heat makes the grass shrivel and burn. The trees flung into space smolder and explode into flame and fall to ash at our feet. Even as a spirit, not truly existing in this time, the intensity of the heat makes me want to touch my hair to see if it has caught fire.

The horizon is aglow and slowly I watch in awe as a giant cloud in the form of a terrible mushroom takes shape. Oh God, I say to myself, an atomic bomb. Someone's exploded an atomic bomb. What happened? Where did this happen? How did it happen? I ask myself those questions and tears fall from my eyes and slide down my face. The Guide comes over and brushes away the saline drops. He beckons me to follow him to another landscape.

"The Jews and Arabs of Israel," the Guide explains, "fought against each other with determination and bravery. Each side committed atrocities so awful that it was not assumed that peace could ever be achieved. But they did achieve peace because wise men interceded and wiser men recognized that there could be peace if they could give it a try."

In other situations the wise men were missing—and misery took the place of making the world a better place. "That cloud," he said, "shows how the failure of man to read the need for peace paves the road to destruction."

That explosion had its roots in the distant past—even before the time of Kateri Tekakwitha, he explained.

"Not as old as the time where I come from, but old, nevertheless," the Guide says.

The origins of that thermonuclear blast are four thousand years old. Two millennia before Jesus came to Nazareth, fierce people occupied the territory north of the Tigris River; these shepherds and mountain hunters even spread into regions of Babylonia. They were called by various names which eventually were corrupted into the term Kurd. The land they occupied was known as Kurdistan.

The Kurds fought every group that tried to dominate them and were employed by the enemy of one to fight a common foe. Throughout their history, the Kurds fought to remain distinct from other groups, refusing to be assimilated as they assimilated others. Yet never through history did the Kurds find the strength of diplomacy to build a nation of their own. At the end of the twentieth century, the closest entity of a Kurdish state was the protected area in northern Iraq where omnipresent United Nations forces kept Kurds safe from the latest madman to attempt to run Iraq.

But there were more Kurds in Iran, in Syria, in the Caucasus, and the most numerous Kurds were in Eastern Turkey. At the end of World War I, a spokesman for the Kurds demanded that Eastern Turkey be set aside as an independent homeland for the Kurds. The request was ignored. The desire for independence for the Kurds festered.

The first formal violence between Kurds and those governments occupying what the Kurds call Kurdistan began in 1925. A Kurdish revolt was crushed by regular Turk armies. Nearly fifty leaders of the Kurdish rebellion were captured, tried and were executed by Turks. But the crackdown never changed the disregard among the Kurds for their own government. The Kurds, the Jews in Israel, and the Palestinians were all in similar boats. Foreigners occupied their lands and there would be no end of the bloodshed until they were either all dead or they had achieved their goal. Palestinians and Jews succeeded in developing their own states. By the eve of the centennial of that first revolution in 1925— in the year 2025—Kurdistan was still a region, a state of mind, but not a state. The millions of Kurds chafed under the rule of others.

That the Kurds and Armenians should become allies in one of the world's most horrifying terrorist actions is strange. For in 1894, Kurds massacred hundreds of Armenians while sacking their villages. But after twenty years of enmity, relations warmed. As Kurds and Armenians struggled to cast off the mantle of hatred, a new problem arose for the Christian Armenians amidst their more populous Turkish-Muslim countrymen.

During the early stages of World War I, Turks decided to physically deport the two million plus Armenians from the country, and in the process raped, tortured, and massacred more than half a million Armenians—some say more than a million died—in one of the world's great atrocities. It is said that Adolph Hitler, noting the lack of world wrath against the Turks, planned his "final solution" for Jews convinced that the world would watch, then turn away and do nothing. For that is precisely what the world did when confronted by the Turkish massacre of the Armenians.

Even expelled, their numbers terribly reduced by the awful Turkish massacres, Armenia still managed to forge an independent nation in the Caucasus Mountains. Then the tiny Armenia was attacked from the south by Turks and from the east by Soviets who had already captured Azerbaijan and independent Armenia disappeared for seventy years until the breakup of the Soviet Union in 1992.

Armenians and Kurds at one time hated each other. Certainly there was never any great love between the Christian Armenians and the Muslim Kurds. But they each hated the Turks. Perhaps their alliance in the terrorist activity they joined in 2010 wasn't so hard to figure out after all: The enemy of my enemy is my friend. Kurds and Armenians held no love for each other, but their individual hatred of Turks was extreme.

Kurdish or Armenian violence against Turks occurred regularly through the twentieth century; the Kurds seeking independence, while the Armenians demanded an apology, even an apology decades late, for the destruction of its people.

Early in the twenty-first century, Kurdish rebels began contacts with clandestine groups of Armenians who continued to demand revenge against the Turks for the deaths of the Armenians' great-grandparents and great nieces and nephews and cousins many times removed. The passage of time failed to heal the putrefying wounds left agape in the Turkish wilderness one hundred years earlier.

These contacts found a method of obtaining weapons-grade enriched uranium that was not accounted for in nuclear energy manufacture. The uranium, arriving in lead containers containing just a few ounces, was smuggled out of the Ukraine, from Siberia, from Kazakhstan. Kurds recruited Kurds who had succeeded in science at foreign universities to begin development of an atomic weapon.

The Armenians provided the Kurds with the uranium only if the Kurds told what the plan was going to be. The Armenians found out the plan and withdrew to await the results, not realizing that putting together a secret nuclear bomb doesn't happen over the weekend. In fact it did not happen for years.

The Armenians wanted the Kurds to explode their weapon in 2015—the anniversary of the Armenian massacres. But 2015 passed, so did 2016 and 2017. In time the Armenian underground forgot what they had unleashed a decade before. But the stateless Kurds remembered.

The bomb was finished in 2023. Now the Kurds began planning how to move the bomb into position. Finally, in early spring of 2025, everything was in place. But

again the Kurds waited. The decision was to explode
the bomb in August, the month when the fifty leaders
of the Kurdish rebellion were executed a hundred years
earlier.

By then, too many people knew of the bomb's existence. Rumors reached the Turkish intelligence community. Some of those who were peripheral members of the
plot "committed suicide" or were murdered by others. At
least three times, Turkish investigators were minutes late
in locating the hiding place of the device. In fact, early
in the year, word of the device leaked to the media, but
the public failed to heed the stories and failed to believe
the stories. Until August 11, 2025.

The plan was to bring the bomb in a truck, close to
the government offices in Ankara, the capital of Turkey. But it was soon obvious that security was too
effective. A thought of abandoning the truck in a poor
neighborhood close to the center of the city is scotched
because of fears that the vehicle will be stripped and
looted before detonation. After riding around for an hour
with the device ticking down, the terrorists will locate
a parking space in downtown Ankara, will load up the
parking meter, and walk away from the disaster.

Just at sundown, the device will explode, incinerating
everything and everyone in a five-square-mile area. Although crude as nuclear devices go, the blast will still
exceed the destruction caused by the bombs at Hiroshima
and Nagasaki combined. The death toll will be estimated
in excess of 780,000 people. Tens of thousands of those
who survive will die within five years of radiation-caused
cancers and leukemias. The bomb will be "dirty" and
radiation will make a fifty-square-mile area around the
initial explosion uninhabitable.

The numbing death toll stuns even the terrorists who
planted the nuclear bomb. They will fail to take credit for
the explosion, but even amateur historians will recognize
that the explosion coincides with the one-hundredth anniversary of the executions of the Kurd martyrs. Authorities

will round up suspects, but no physical evidence will exist that can result in trials. Even when circumstantial evidence points the finger toward Armenia, authorities will still be forced to admit that they have no clues or evidence or even any statements from reliable witnesses that will lead to finding fault.

Eventually, the government of Turkey will submit that the explosion was the work of unnamed and unconvicted Kurdish terrorists who do not have the sanction of the Kurdish people. No mention of the Armenian connection will ever be made by the government of Turkey. However, in a statement in the Turkish parliament at the rebuilt capital of the rebuilt city of Ankara in 2044, the government of Turkey will formally apologize to the people of Armenia for the atrocities committed to the Armenians in 1915–16.

As has happened so many times in the past, the action of a few militant Kurds will affect the rest of the nation. Kurd nationalism will be dealt a death blow in Turkey. Anyone espousing Kurdish independence will be shouted down or pummeled to near death by ferocious mobs of Turks. There will be no escaping the wrath of the Turkish majority. In Syria and Iran, Kurds will be hounded into ghettos from which they will not emerge for the remainder of the century.

Only in the tiny Kurdish enclave in Iraq will Kurds exist with some form of self-government, but only as long as UN forces protect them.

I looked at the blackened earth, a scattered few timbers of twisted metal and concrete rods protruding from the black ash. "There must be something that can be done to prevent this," I protested.

"Of course there is," the Guide agreed. "But who will take your words to heart. So many times have warnings been given—and so many times the people in charge have not done what has to be done to change what has to be changed.

"Your message opens the lock on the book of the

future. But will they read? And if they read, will they act to change this dire forecast or will they ignore it and say 'Folly,' as so many other have said.

"The ink has not yet set on the pages of history. Once the ink is dry, the time to edit the future and the lives of millions of people will pass—into oblivion."

10

ASTEROIDS

CAREFULLY BALANCING THE BAG OF GROCERIES ON ONE hip, I put the key into the lock of my apartment's front door, turned the key, and entered. The apartment should have been empty, and, I suppose, to everyone but me it would have appeared empty.

A half-naked man squatted on the floor, carefully perusing a map of the Far East. A year ago I would have screamed, tossed the groceries in the air, and ran back to the street hoping to find that cop who was always writing parking tickets to place under the windshield wiper on my automobile. (Why do I have an automobile in New York City? Why do hundreds of thousands of people have automobiles? None of us know why; we all have reasons, but none of us really know why. Maybe it's because there has to be a place to put all those parking tickets.)

But today, I barely glanced at the Guide. Instead I just shifted the bag of food in my arms, closed the door, threw the locks, and marched to the kitchen to put away my purchases. "What do you find so interesting in the atlas?" I called to the Guide.

"I'm trying to find the valley where the last battle of the Great War was fought."

I walked back into the living room and peered over his shoulder. "You are looking at a map of India," I said. "The Great War—World War I—was fought in Europe."

He shook his head, and answered with disdain. "No, I'm talking about the Great War between China and India in 2022, the one the United States ended with its great Thunderclap secret weapon."

I smiled at him. "Oh, that war."

He almost smiled—had I ever seen him smile?—as he played along. "Nice recovery. Yes, that war. You know, the one in which twenty-eight million people died before anyone in the West thought it was worth worrying about?"

I visibly blanched. (In this day of CNN how could a tragedy of that magnitude occur without anyone becoming upset by it? Would we be so used to death in vast numbers that twenty-eight million bodies would have no effect?) I carried on gamely. "Yes, of course, that Great War. I'm a bit hazy on it however. Could you refresh my memory?"

He stood and stretched his six-foot-tall body. As he extended his arms, I distinctly heard his elbow and shoulder joints pop—a singularly bizarre achievement for an apparition. A shudder went through me as I realized that this apparition was able to remove books from my shelves and turn pages of the atlas. I slid that thought into my subconscious and traipsed after the Guide to the table where my notebook of automatic writings was kept. I watched in awe as the pages turned by themselves until it stopped at a portion of the notebook filled with unintelligible scrawls.

"You were writing in Chinese," the Guide explained, pointing to some stick figure-style strokes. "And here you were writing in Hindi." He gestured to other letters which might as well have been Greek or Hebrew or Arabic. He smirked: "It's all there. You've written it already. I guess you don't need my help."

I sighed to myself, "Only you, Shawn, could have found a sarcastic ghost." I told the Guide, "Humor me, please."

Instantly, my safe, quiet—as quiet as it gets in New York's Greenwich Village—home melted away and I stood in a snowdrift in the Himalayas. It's a strange sensation to be wearing slacks and a blouse and be standing in two feet of snow—and not be physically chilled.

"The Chinese had to cross these mountains and this plateau to attack India. The Nepalese were no contest and no impediment. No one wants to get in the way of a couple of million soldiers," the Guide said.

The buildup to the war between India and China had been in the making for generations. But it was China's refusal at the end of the twentieth century to cease nuclear bomb experiments that led to the road to war between the world's most populous nations.

The Chinese decision to continue bomb experimentation was met by disapproval from the United States, but China found itself in a difficult world position. Still clinging—officially—to communism, the Chinese felt themselves ostracized from the rest of the world. It was surrounded by neighbors with powerful weapons, huge populations, and alien cultures. To the north and east was Russia, still struggling with the pitfalls of developing democracy, but still armed with thousands of nuclear weapons and hundreds of missiles that could deliver the weapons. To China's northwest was Korea, an alleged ally, but terribly unstable with an unpopular leadership. Not only was North Korea unstable, it also had its own cache of nuclear devices.

To the south was Vietnam, now an emerging economic and political power since it renewed relations with the United States. Vietnam was nuclear-free, but the nation supported the largest standing army in southeast Asia and was a traditional enemy of China. And to the southwest was the one billion people of India and one hundred million Pakistanis—and both countries were nuclear-armed to the teeth.

Tensions grew strained when, in 2008, India quadrupled the number of troops in the northeast section of the nation. India claimed that it needed the troops to quell an impending rebellion by natives of India's Nagaland district—an area of unrest for fifty years. The Chinese thought that India was using Nagaland as an excuse to load up an area in dispute between India and China. The Chinese noted with alarm that in the second half of the twentieth century the most imperialistic of all the nations in the world was India.

The Chinese remembered how India invaded and absorbed the Portuguese colony of Goa in the 1950s; then swallowed Sikkim in the 1980s; created a virtual servile state out of independent Bhutan; reduced Nepal into a near "protected" status; humbled Pakistan in a series of conflicts; and made many in Bangladesh—surrounded on three sides by Indian territory—insecure as India tightened an economic noose around the impoverished nation of 130 million people living in an area the size of Wisconsin.

China, of course, was the nation with the world's largest population—pushing one and a quarter billion by 2010. It also had a major nuclear arsenal and the means to deliver the weapons of mass destruction. Border skirmishes began around 2015—an exact date is hard to determine because neither side bothered to report the incursions since both sides were violating ceasefire agreements. The nations continually rattled their nuclear weapons, but the thought of using weapons of mass destruction was blunted by the realization that if one nation used the nuclear bomb others would retaliate with the same type of weapon. Everyone also realized that there was strong resolve to use nuclear weapons if the other side used them. They were faced with a hellish standoff.

Instead, the Chinese and Indians fought each other with the best alternative weapon at hand—their incredible masses of people. Soldiers, some armed only with sabers or machetes, formed armies of millions and rushed at each other in close fighting. It was bloody and nasty, but it didn't contaminate the earth. No one outside of the immediate area paid any attention to the extent of the devastation.

The method of choice of attack was simply to denude the landscape and the population through mass attack. Thousands of soldiers clashed in close fighting as troops battled each other mainly with small arms. An occasional tank or two got involved in the attacks, and aircraft overhead indiscriminately bombed both military and civilian targets. In general, the rest of the world yawned, beset by other problems and not inclined to get involved in a decades-old dispute. Millions of people died, but the loss of millions among billions of people in remote areas had little impact on the antagonists.

Escalation of the war, however, reached the concerns of the United Nations in 2020, when the alleged sovereignty of Nepal was threatened by China. The Chinese figured that Nepal's sovereignty was moot, since three hundred thousand Indian troops had been "protecting" the country for twenty years. From their vantage point in Nepal, Indian troops had been harassing Chinese troop formations in Tibet. The Chinese had troops there in attempts to keep the local populace from revolting as they had in 1952. After more than fifty years, China still hadn't succeeded in stamping out the embers of independence in the Tibetans.

In 2021, China began bringing more than two million troops to Tibet. The troops marched at the rate of fifteen miles a day to the frontiers of the country. Two million soldiers weren't brought to Tibet to keep the locals in line. It was obvious that China was planning a thrust into Nepal, then across the Himalayas, and then to send the tens of thousands troops into the heart of

India. You can't move two million troops by foot and expect to surprise anyone. India began to move masses of its troops into place. In early 2021, open hostilities broke out. Airplanes from both sides bombed the menacing armies of the other—and when the armies couldn't be located, the planes bombed crowded cities. The three hundred thousand Indian troops in Nepal were overmatched. The native Nepalese retreated to their homes and waved, smiling as the Chinese marched across their narrow homeland.

As India prepared to meet the Chinese troop movement, Chinese diplomacy created a serious problem for India's flanks. The Chinese signed nonaggression treaties with both Pakistan and Bangladesh, and those two Moslem countries began arming their borders with India. India was especially concerned about Pakistan, a nation it had defeated three times in previous wars. But Pakistan was still a potent enemy and that nation began rattling its sabers and talking about reclaiming disputed territory in Kashmir.

A nervous United Nations, recognizing that there were half a dozen countries or potential combatants in this local war—the total death count was way over twenty million but that didn't seem to faze anyone—recognized that the odds of that long-awaited Third World War occurring were getting shorter and shorter, and decided to intervene.

The combatants noted the UN's concern, dismissed it, and went ahead with their own plans to cause mass destruction amongst their enemies. The Chinese troops began driving down the sides of the Himalayas, fighting against monsoon rains, poor roads, and peasants armed with pitchforks and hoes. The Indians moved more than three million soldiers to oppose the Chinese in the valleys south of the mountains. Simultaneously, Pakistanis crossed the border and began attacking Indian troops in Kashmir. Noncombatants in the paths of the armies were obliterated. The death tolls reached unthinkable numbers; atrocities occurred too often to be recorded.

Rivers ran with blood; the sky was obscured by the smoke of burning houses and businesses.

But worse was that India was losing the war. Indian troops were being pushed backward yard by yard, mile by mile. Caught in a multifront war with multiple enemies—even Burma began making incursions in the east—India's military leaders began demanding that they be allowed to used "tactical" nuclear weapons to stop the attacks on its territory. The civilian government resisted, knowing full well that India didn't have tactical nuclear weapons, just basic bombs that would turn cities into concave, blackened pits. India's politicians also knew that the tactical weapons of China and Pakistan would similarly turn cities of the Indian subcontinent into black bowls that glowed in the night.

Indian emissaries made secret trips to the UN, pleading that the UN end the warfare before the Indian military loosed the nuclear power on their enemies. Recognizing that multiple nuclear explosions were not only unhealthy for China, India, and Pakistan—but that the fallout would devastate Bangladesh, Southeast Asia, Japan, and much of the rest of the northern hemisphere, the UN began working with its most powerful members—especially the US—on a plan to end hostilities.

The UN decreed that enough was enough and authorized the United States to take action. The US told the warring parties that if there wasn't peace in forty-eight hours, the US would unleash a secret weapon that it began to develop when Ronald Reagan was president.

The warring parties involved in hand-to-hand combat along a two-hundred-mile line of hostilities pondered for a very short time the consequences of facing this "secret" weapon. They then ignored the UN and scoffed at this unknown force that has been kept safely under wraps for forty years.

The UN extended the warning twice more, and then ten days later the US struck—from space. Although space was supposed to be weapons-free, United States military chiefs had convinced a succession of presidents to violate the international space treaties. Without telling anyone, including its own people, the US not only had been placing weapons in space, it had used its superior technology to find weapons of other nations in orbit and systematically destroy them. At one point France objected to this operation but realizing that they were overmatched technologically, militarily, and legally, even the French kept quiet about violations of the treaty. About the only countries who didn't violate the weapons in space treaty were nations that hadn't been able to launch space satellites.

While the US had a number of antisatellite weapons available—and most governments knew they were there—only a very limited number of highly placed government leaders and intelligence agency knew about the most fearsome weapon ever devised: the Thunderclap.

When the answer to attack was given, a satellite was maneuvered into place twenty-two thousand miles above the Himalayas. Silently and secretly, a series of orbs were launched from the satellite. The computer-driven balls of scientifically constructed alloys drove through the atmosphere virtually unscathed by friction of the air. Even so, the speed of the descending orbs in the atmosphere created streaks of light that could be seen in the night sky as meteors. To avoid that, the spheres were launched in daylight to prevent anyone from spotting their entry into the skies over India.

Traveling at speeds in excess of ten thousand miles an hour, the spheres descended until they were just two miles above the battlefields and scorched earth of northern India. Orbs were situated about twenty-five miles apart along the areas of conflict between Indians and Chinese and Indians and Pakistanis. Without warning the spheres exploded simultaneously. The fearsome detonations created monstrous convulsions in the atmosphere: Wave after wave after wave of intense sonic blasts were directed downward to the earth. The shock and sound waves deafened or knocked unconscious every living organism for fifty miles in every direction. Hostilities ceased instantly since no one could stand upright; no one could hear because the eruptions from the orbs caused instant, though reversible deafness. The waves of sound disrupted all communications, making it impossible for anyone to discuss military operations with anyone else. The shocks so battered the people that they became exhausted from the constant pummeling. The sonic eruptions continued for hours. When the waves finally stopped after six deafening hours, troops from both sides started looking for anyone who looked like an official so they could surrender. The soldiers—and many civilians as well—later said that they had never known so much pain and realized instantly that no combat was worth that pain—no goal, no territory, no prize could be given to make them suffer that agony again. In theory, Thunderclap was designed to immobilize and subdue enemy forces and not to cause fatalities; nor was Thunderclap supposed to be able to destroy property. In reality, anyone who suffered from heart disease or other frailties died during the horrendous assault. The death toll from Thunderclap was in the tens of thousands (naturally, military experts later determined that the use of the device really saved a lot of lives despite the "unfortunate" losses due to "suboptimal physiques" of the peasant farmers, their elderly parents, and young children). Buildings collapsed from the vibrations, especially the structures built without the best of materials— virtually everything in the combat areas.

With military forces in disarray, another ultimatum was issued by the United Nations. The Chinese, Indian, and Pakistani governments, of course, said they would study the proposals. An hour after their study began, the satellite released three more spheres—one overhead at New Delhi, another above Beijing, and a third was dispatched over Islamabad. The ultimatum expired at noon. At 12:01 PM, the spheres exploded. Ten hours later, a new ultimatum was issued by the United Nations. All the factions agreed to end hostilities, recall their troops, and settle differences by arbitration. The UN gave the parties until January 1, 2025 to determine final boundaries and settle all issues outstanding between the parties. The US announced that by that time, it would have a new, improved version of Thunderclap ready for use. The agreements were signed with eight months to spare.

The Thunderclap was hailed as the weapon to end weapons, but no one believed that. Military experts explained that the Thunderclap was forty years old, and the US and other technologically advanced nations— read Japan, the Ukraine Axis, and the European Common Market here—were no doubt developing their own weapons that could render Thunderclap useless or at least be more powerful than this weapon.

Thunderclap ended hostilities between armies on the move, but it didn't eliminate nuclear arsenals. Interestingly, none of the combatants in the India-China-Pakistan battles insisted that anything be done about nuclear weapons. Everyone held onto their A bombs.

And it was a good thing that they did.

11

ASTEROIDS 2

THE GUIDE LIFTED THE HALF-GALLON CARTON OF Tropicana orange juice and poured it into a tall glass commemorating the first year of the Florida Marlins—"Wait till I tell you about real expansion in baseball," he said—and took a long swallow. I waited for the juice to spill to the floor. But it didn't. He looked at me and said, "Don't worry about it. You know almost nothing about us." He put the glass down and walked through the wall of the apartment. "Nope, it hasn't been raining," he said as he walked back into the room through the wall again. "Time is the key. Remember that. It's the fourth dimension."

Eventually my mouth closed and I remembered the Sino-Indian War story, and the Guide's closing pronouncement that it was a good thing that the warring nations didn't get rid of their atomic weapons.

"Naturally," he explained, "when India and China and Pakistan kept their nuclear arsenal, do did England, France, Russia, Ukraine, and everyone else. If there was one nation that had the big bomb, then everyone wanted it 'as a deterrent.' "

The Guide shook his head. "Deterrence. Ha! Since nations have had the atomic bomb the only deterrence had been that no one has dared use the bomb. That hasn't stopped anyone from going to war. Look around the world today in your time and count the wars: Bosnians fighting Serbs and Croats; Croats fighting Serbs; Arabs fighting Israelis; Abkhasians fighting Georgians; Azerbaijanis fighting Armenians; Kurds battling Turks and Iraqis; Iraqis fighting Iranis and Kuwaitis; Peruvians fighting each other; Angolans in civil war; Burmese harassing Bangladeshis; India and Pakistan in disputes; Afghans emerged in civil conflict; Guatemalans threatening Belize; brushfires breaking out in Liberia, Ghana, Uganda, Rwanda, Burundi, Mozambique, Somalia, Egypt. The list is endless. Deterrence hasn't worked and never will work but everyone had to have the bomb.

"Of course without the bomb civilization would have ended in 2045 when the asteroids would have clawed the earth to bits, gouging huge swathes across continents and crashing into the oceans, causing massive tidal waves that virtually wiped out all coastal cities and towns.

"But thanks to the bomb that didn't happen."

The speech by the Guide was eloquent, but I told him that I wasn't following his thoughts. "Right now, is the start of the end of the world. You are living the end of the world right now. Only a few people really are speculating on what is happening that has the very real potential of destroying everything we know. Even as we talk those changes are taking place—on Jupiter."

He pointed to the ceiling, which vanished, and a picture of the giant planet Jupiter swam into view. We were watching the planet as if we were looking through a giant telescope or were standing on one of Jupiter's moons. "Over there—see that formation," he nudged me. I could see what looked to be falling rocks streaking toward the far side of the planet. "That's the remains of a comet—Shoemaker-Levy 9—which is only about a mile or two wide. In early 1992 the comet came so close to Jupiter that it caused massive tidal disturbances on the planet. In 1994, what was left of the comet hit the planet itself," he explained.

Interesting, I thought, but does it have any meaning to me? To earth—fifty years later?

The Guide took me closer to the planet's surface. "See that," he said. I squinted at the end of his finger and I thought I could see something emerge from the methane-covered surface of the planet and fly off into space. "Sure," I said. "What's that?"

"That, dear Shawn, is the end of civilization." I recalled my notes. "Streaks of light," I had written. "Destruction at night." The Guide nodded affirmatively. "Those are the clues."

I looked again at Jupiter and the few streaks emerging from the planet. It didn't look like much to me. We drew back from the planet. The Guide showed me how that speck of debris, only about eight hundred yards in length, but particularly dense, would begin a course that would create havoc on Earth. The small speck of planetary debris bounced into several other similar pieces of cosmic rocks in Jupiter's rings. It created a Ping-Pong effect. As each rock was knocked out of its precise orbit, it struck other rocks, knocking them astray. Soon one hundred rocks, many larger than the initial one, were careering out of control. In Ping-Pong and mousetrap experiments, Ping-Pong balls explode all over the place in seconds. In the cosmic redux of the experiment, it took years before anyone noticed anything was amiss.

The first hints of problems occurred in 2010 when a student at the University of Arizona, doing a simple assignment on the orbits of the major moons of Jupiter, kept coming up with the wrong data. In fact, his data indicated that the orbits of both Io and Ganymede were changing. Since this was a student, no one paid much

attention to his problem—in fact, his professor repri-
manded him and gave him a new astronomical puzzle
to work out.

A year later, when a second student also reported
to the professor that he couldn't resolve the orbits of
the moons, the professor himself looked into the problem. To his surprise, he realized that his first student
was right. Now he could see that the orbits of the two
moons had changed—and the change was radical. He
plotted what the new orbits meant and he stunned the
world by predicting that within ten years the two moons
would collide.

Confirmation of his published data came quickly as
excited scientists around the globe began watching the
pending showdown in the skies. The scientific community in the world lobbied hard and successfully to get
an international expedition mounted so that a base could
be established on Callisto, the largest of the Jupiter's
moons in a stable orbit. Although prepared hastily, the
expedition managed to get to Callisto and set up an
observatory about a year before impact was predicted
in 2021.

The collision was the CNN event of the year. For two
straight days CNN cameras watched in awe as the two
moons drifted closer and closer. Experts discussed the
possibilities that the gravitational fields of the moons
would change their orbits enough to avoid a collision,
but the speculation became moot when the moons hit—
both of them disintegrated before the watchful cameras.
The "Sudden Impact in Space" was replayed thousands
of times—an instant replay of the century.

Scientists who had predicted the collisions—that
much-maligned University of Arizona student was
awarded the $2.2 million Nobel Prize—became celeb-
rities, talking about how they worked out the details
that proved how well science could predict events in
space. But while they were reaping the rewards of the
rubber chicken circuit, other scientists were gnashing

their teeth as they aimed powerful telescopes at Jupiter and the asteroid belt.

They warned that not all was well; that the addition of thousands of new asteroids would mess up the orbits of other asteroids and that could create a chain reaction that would send the space rocks on a fatal collision course with the Earth. At first they were decried as Cassandras, but their warnings soon were believed: The moons didn't crumble to dust in the violent collision in space, they were just splintered into billions of particles, some miles wide. And these new asteroids were bouncing through the Asteroid Belt, knocking other minor planets off course and out of their traditional orbits. The new orbits passed through Earth's orbit. Chunks of stone a couple of miles in length and width would not be consumed in the atmosphere. They would crash to the Earth and create massive destruction which hadn't occurred in millennia—not since dinosaurs ruled the earth.

In 2038, a new breed of astronomers, meteor early-warning watchers or MEW2s were scanning the heavens and plotting scenarios of what was expected to be an onslaught of meteors. The MEW2s' first warning in 2040 was for a quarter-mile-long iron rock that was tumbling in a direct intercept course with earth. One of the first suggested ways of handling the meteor was to send up a rocket tipped with a nuclear bomb and reduce it to radioactive ash.

That met with international hemming and hawing. There were moralists on every side of the issue—some said that we should let God's will be done; others suggested that God's will be damned, we had to protect our planet; others pooh-poohed the calculations of the scientists; and still others expected that the earth's protective atmosphere would make quick work of the asteroid and would reduce it to ash or tiny particles.

On October 30, 2040, during one of the driest spells on record in Washington state, that quarter-mile-long meteor entered the atmosphere of earth. The friction between the meteor and the air caused the huge rock to superheat and melt and even burn. In fact almost a third of the rock, it was estimated, had disintegrated when, glowing brightly enough to turn darkened Seattle into day and roaring through the sonic barrier, the meteor sliced a two-hundred-mile crease across the Sierra Nevada Mountains before cratering itself west of Spokane. It took six months to put out all the forest fires caused by the streaking meteorite. The death toll was surprisingly small—officially put at 280 people (another one hundred people were killed fighting the fires or trying to escape fire-fighting equipment which raced to one blaze after another). The first lesson in the Battle of the Asteroids had begun. The score was Asteroid 1, Earth 0. The MEW2s now reported that they had at least fifteen more asteroids in sight that were going to strike the Earth within the next decade. They were most worried about MEW2s-16, a fifteen-mile-wide chunk of planet— believed to be part of Ganymede—that was heading our way. Earth-ending calamity was assured if this rock landed in anyone's backyard.

Now the idea of using atomic bombs to force the asteroids off course or to vaporize them stopped becoming a moral issue. The scarred, blackened surface of central Washington was all anyone had to recall to realize that no weapon was immoral if it could save the planet. Out from secret hiding places and storehouses and silos came the weapons of mass destruction. There were thousands of rocks up there that were threatening earth and even with nuclear overkill, there might not be enough bombs on earth to save the planet. Long-moth-balled nuclear weapons plants were renovated on emergency bases as the number-one priority around the world was to build more bombs.

Space shuttles were being loaded to maximum tolerances to take the bombs to the space stations where daring Asteroid Cowboys—the world's newest heroes—

strapped the bombs to small craft and flew into harm's way between the Earth and Mars. Using tracking information from Earth, the two-man spaceships would maneuver towards an asteroid. Then one crewman would manhandle the bomb to the speeding asteroid. Speed of course was relative as the rock, the shuttle, and the spacewalking crewman were all traveling the same speed—in excess of seventeen thousand miles per hour. The tricky part was getting a foothold on the asteroids, some of which were spinning or tumbling through the weightlessness of space. Then came the problem of securing the bomb on the asteroid, setting a suitable fuse time, and getting the hell away from the asteroid before it was blown to kingdom come. All of this was watched on earth by the ever-present news cameras that were sent by remote control from every national TV station as well as the privately controlled media outlets such as CNN. Once the crewman set the fuse he hightailed it as fast as his Flash Gordon packs would take him to his pathetically small spaceship. The Cowboys' ships were often tiny compared to the news media monster spacecraft. Once back to the ship, it was time for the ship to make tracks—or at least ion trails—away from the asteroid. The first attempt to blow one up worked without a snag. The explosion, however, was a disappointment to the television audience. Mushroom clouds don't occur in space. There was just a brilliant flash and then a lot of debris. Ratings for asteroid disintegrations dropped precipitously.

The MEW2s were now able to establish forward telescopic observatories on satellites that were moved further from earth and closer to Mars so that earlier warnings of threatening rocks could be made. The Cowboys became adept at blowing up the rocks with the nuclear bombs, but larger mini-moons were still worrisome to scientists who weren't sure that a single explosion would suffice in reducing objects such as MEW2s-16 to microscopic and nonthreatening dust. Simulations indicated that nuclear explosions might just cause the rock to calve, and break into two or three still deadly stones. And they also realized that once one nuclear strike had been made on an asteroid there could not be another. The rock would be too radioactively hot for anyone, no matter the level of spacesuit protection, to secure another bomb on the surface of the asteroid. Firing weapon-tipped missiles at the larger rocks was considered impractical because there wasn't enough control to make sure the bombs hit where they would do the most good.

But as MEW2s-16 closed in on its encounter with Earth, scientists decided to blast the rock anyway, in hopes of at least changing its course. If MEW2s missed Earth, it was calculated that the planet would be spared another encounter for at least seventy-five years. The problem this time was to make sure that the explosion would knock the asteroid off course in the right direction. So critical was the need to position the explosion correctly that a team of scientists accompanied the top Asteroid Cowboys on the mission in the summer of 2045. The team caught up with the asteroid when it was a mere sixteen million miles from Earth. They were delighted to find that the orb spun slowly, which allowed the teams to gain a secure foothold. They were able to anchor the nuclear device precisely in place. The scientists waited two days after the device was in place before exploding it, to make sure the explosion occurred at exactly the right time during MEW2s's spin so it would hurl the huge stone into a new path. The explosion, however, had to take place when the scientists were dangerously close to the asteroid. If they moved too far away the detonating signal would take a fraction too long to reach the bomb and would throw off the calculations. For all the scientific effort and all the computer knowledge that went into the MEW2s-16 episode, top scientists later agreed that it was just one big crap shoot.

In fact, there was significant error in the crap shoot. The nearness to the explosion meant that many of the scientists' equipment was useless for days and weeks after the explosion. As the world held its breath, the scientists realized that they had only changed the course of the rock slightly. It would still pass within ten thousand miles of earth. Ten thousand miles might seem like a long distance, but it was far too close for comfort for those who knew the dynamics of space and how much damage the rock could do if it hit the planet. Now the question was: would the Earth's own gravitational pull grab the rock and prove that God was stronger than man? The huge stone whipped by the Earth, causing panic when it streaked past a full moon and was witnessed by tens of millions of people. But the rock kept on going, sparing the planet—this time.

The success in being able to change the course of the satellites with bombs now resulted in other ideas for dealing with the stones. Giant nuclear-fueled jet engines were manufactured on Earth and were sent into space. The Asteroid Cowboys took the engines to threatening rocks, bolted the engines in place, and set the engines running. By placing two of the engines on each asteroid, scientists on the moon, Mars, or the space stations could change the orbits just by firing one engine. So the same bombs which were believed to be the eventual destruction of mankind, actually became its savior.

"The lesson that mankind must learn but probably never will learn is that mankind really knows not what it is doing," the Guide said.

12

KEVORKIAN CAMPS

I SCRUTINIZED MY AUTOMATIC WRITINGS, TRYING TO decipher my scribbling. One series of notes caught my attention. I tried to concentrate on the words. Images danced before my eyes. I saw faces; I could hear screams of anguish but times and dates were vague. I couldn't focus on the event.

The process of interpreting psychic dreams goes this route. Sometimes I would think: "Aha, this is what is going on." And everything would fit. But with these notes, nothing seemed to fit. I was looking at a lot of round pegs and my board only had square holes. There were moments when I believed I had a solution, but then the view would fade and distort and I couldn't be sure at all that I had any clue. With these writings I had come to depend on my Guide for assistance. I knew he could help me across these canyons of doubts.

Now I looked upon the riddle on my desk. "People. Death. Joy. Blood. 'Leave us alone.' Woods." I closed my eyes and images jumped to the television screen that played in my mind. I could see what seemed to me to be mobs attacking a barricade; blocks which I thought represented authority figures pushed the mobs back. And behind the blocks were scores of frail, sickly rabbits huddled around trees and shrubs seeking protection. "Metaphors," I mumbled to myself, "but what do they represent?"

I watched in detached fascination as explosions emerged from all sides and figures fell prostrate to the ground, a redness oozing from them. Obviously, violence and bloodshed were occurring, but I couldn't grab the essence of the scene. Here was a portrayal of something of importance but I couldn't come up with a date, a time, or a place. I felt as if I were in Russia, watching a movie when all the conversation was in a language I couldn't understand.

This, of course, is of great frustration to a psychic. Here I was receiving a message from a powerful source. I was seeing the future—how, I don't dare try to explain even to myself—yet I couldn't tell what all this symbolism meant. I needed help. I needed my Guide. I called for him out loud. I mentally demanded that he come to help me. But he would not appear.

I recalled his warnings.

He told me, "I may seem magical to you and you may believe that I an omniscient or that I have superpowers. That's not true. It's not that easy to travel between dimensions and time and through the spirit world. There are times I will be delayed; there will be times when simple atmospherics—such as static electricity—will prevent me from coming to you. There will be some time in the future when you will call me or need me or see something that requires an explanation, and I will not be able to appear. I cannot be your guide forever. In fact my time with you will seem too short even when it is far too long. Others call me in other times requiring my assistance. We Guides are not many, and some are not as strong at reaching those such as yourself. I will help you as long as possible, but even for me as long as possible is a limited period indeed."

What was worse to me was the fear that I'd never know when the Guide would be making his final visit. He told me he didn't know either. I'd have no hint that he was gone. He didn't appear every hour or every day; he didn't respond to my requests to appear and help. He just showed up—sometimes when I wasn't even thinking about the writings or the visions. I only knew that I'd have to use his knowledge whenever he was available.

I shuddered as I recalled his warnings about his own shortcomings, especially now as I struggled to find meaning with these visions. Am I now alone with these clues? I thought. I looked around the room and spotted the medal I had purchased at Auriesville. "It's a third-class relic," the woman had told me. She explained that the little piece of cloth attached to the medal of Kateri Tekakwitha had touched another object which had been in contact with the actual bones of the woman who someday could become the first Native American to be named a saint. I closed my fist over the medal. I didn't pray. I just held it in my palm. And then I put it back on the desk next to my loose-leaf notebook of automatic writings.

It had been days since I had heard from the Guide. I wondered, Is this all there is? Am I on my own now? Can I read the signs well enough to provide the warning necessary?

I continued to struggle with the writings and my limited visions. Something told me that I had the basis of something important. I turned on a strobe light and closed my eyes again. The electronic flashes penetrated my eyelids. I could feel myself going deeply into a trance. The images were getting clearer. I inhaled the acrid stench of gunpowder, and in my mind I could hear screams of pain and anger.

Suddenly, a voice boomed behind my eyes, but not in my ears:

"Turn off that awful light. It's driving me nuts."

I opened my eyes and there was that wonderful Guide, his weathered hand protecting his face from the high-intensity blinking light. His face and body moved in rapid jerks in time with the strobe flashes in the otherwise darkened room. I turned the switch and the lights abruptly stopped. I groped in the corner and flipped on a lamp and glanced at the time. I had turned the light on just after 4 PM. It was now midnight. I'd been in the trance for eight hours and I had picked up about two minutes of usable visions. I was shocked at how long I was in the trance and how little I'd achieved—and I realized I was starving.

The Guide, as usual, was one thought ahead of me and motioned towards the refrigerator. I took out some cold chicken and offered him a piece. He shook his head and rolled his eyes as if to say, "Don't you know that apparitions don't eat?" Sheepishly I devoured the chicken leg, and began sipping a cup of coffee. I started to light a cigarette, but the Guide's stern, forbidding countenance made me return the cigarette to its pack. The adrenaline running through my body—a hormonal burst that occurred whenever he appeared—overcame (temporarily) my body's craving for nicotine.

I pored over my notes again and was about to ask the Guide for help when abruptly I found myself standing in the middle of a riot. Thousands of people were shouting and chanting and carrying signs. They seemed to be moving as a solid mass directly at me. I ducked for cover behind a uniformed policeman who was holding his baton in one hand and slapping it into the other. He looked confident, but the aura of fear surrounded him and the others in the thin line of less than fifty men in blue. I looked over my shoulder at the rustic-style fence behind me. It stretched for what looked like a hundred yards to my left. To my right was a large swinging gate, closed and barricaded with vehicles. The fence of logs ran off to the right another hundred yards or so. I could see a number of people inside the compound, standing on porches of log cabins. They looked nervous and ill and generally seemed elderly.

Suddenly the policeman I was hiding behind jerked violently. An ear-shattering report instantly followed. The policeman gasped and fell to his knees and then crumbled backward to the ground, blood spurting from his chest. Shouts erupted from every direction. I saw guns being aimed at the police from the crowd and tried to warn the police, but they too already had their weapons ready and were blasting away at the crowd that now surged towards them. Their fire was returned from somewhere in the mob. Half a dozen people in the crowd collapsed onto the ground. The mob paused for an instant, but then reeled directly at the police; as more gunfire sounded some people in the rear of the mob turned and began running away or flopped on the ground and covered their heads as if they were trying to ward off blows. Others were knocked to the ground and trampled by the horde. The front ranks of the crowd began wrestling with the policemen in mortal hand-to-hand combat. With their numbers overwhelming the police, the crowd pushed past the police and assaulted the fence. Policemen were being kicked and trampled; their weapons were taken from them and turned on them as they lay helpless on the ground. I became aware of news media at the fringes of the mob, taking still photographs and using miniature videotape recorders to capture the carnage. Some of the reporters fell, too—some in fear and some because the mob turned on them. The crowd attacked the gates almost as if it was a single-minded organism. It swarmed like a mass of bees or locusts and attacked the barricaded gate, which was woefully inadequate to stop the onslaught.

Wood was wrenched from the gate, the hinges popped free, and the gate was hurled to the ground. The frenzied mob began scampering over the cars and carts and trucks that made up the makeshift barricade. One man stood on the roof of a dented sedan and raised his arm in triumph and as a signal for the mob to move forward. And then he vanished as the earth shuddered from the force of a massive explosion that was centered in the car on which the man was standing. The barricade had been booby-trapped. In a twinkling, the cars and trucks were turned into white-hot shrapnel that gutted the mob or enveloped them in flames. The explosion tore the heart out of the demonstrators and left more than 140 of them dead or dying. Scores more were injured. Left dangling from its position atop the gate was the sign that used to hang peacefully over the forested compound. Only one side remained attached as the sign swung slowly back and forth. I craned my head to read it: KEVORKIAN CAMP, SALMON RIVER, IDAHO.

I had just enough time to grasp the meaning of the sign when the horror of the bloodshed disappeared. I was now strolling in a woodland paradise, the guide gently walking with me, holding my elbow as we negotiated the leaf-strewn path.

"The Kevorkian Riot of 2033. That's what you saw. That's what your vision was all about," the Guide told me. We sat on a bench hewn from a log and watched squirrels chase each other in the canopy of leaves overhead. And slowly I learned the history of the Kevorkian Riot.

The camp was named after Dr. Jack Kevorkian, the Michigan physician who received acclaim and acrimony for assisting people who wanted to die to commit suicide. Long after Kevorkian's own problems in the legal system were disposed of—and long after Kevorkian himself had died (of natural causes), many organizations adapted his philosophy: People had the right to die and to choose their death rather than submit to pain-racked existences created by life-extending therapies that kept you alive but weren't life-enhancing.

By the year 2020, there were tens of thousands of Americans and Western Europeans who were living to be 80, 90, 100, 110 years old and were faced with living for decades in pain and failing health. Science was able to find new chemotherapies to keep cancer at bay—but not cure the patient. To stay alive cancer patients—which now included one of every two people over age 80 (medicine was so advanced the only thing you could die of was cancer)—were faced with a regimen of taking chemotherapy and being sick for 50 percent of the time, and not feeling very good the other 50 percent. Life had become an existence; a terrible, ruthless joke—you will be sick for years, and then you'll die.

To the millions of people who fell into this category, organizations such as the Hemlock Society started to look very good. The societies were able to recruit thousands of members, mostly people who were dying slow, agonizing deaths and couldn't look forward to the peace of death for decades. We knew how to keep people who were immobilized by broken bones—suffered in their ninth decade—from developing life-ending diseases such as unhealed cold sores or pneumonias, but we didn't have any way of making their lives worth living.

In 2028, the first Hemlock Society "preparation" camp was opened. The camps were named in honor of Dr. Kevorkian, who had become an icon to the suicide-option minded. Naturally, the first camp opened in southern Sweden, where opposition to such ideas was particularly low. The camps were carved out of forested areas and were built with two purposes in mind: to give the terminally ill a place to reside and live with their friends and family before their health became so intolerable that they would choose to die—in any number of simple and effective and reasonably painless ways. Their suicides were monitored by their loved ones and by doctors who made sure that death came peacefully to their sides.

The rules for admission to the Kevorkian camps were simple: You checked in without any life-extending medications—painkillers were not only permitted, they were dispensed by the camp doctors on request. You signed a will and a declaration that you intended to stay in the camp until you felt too ill to continue and then you would select you own method of departure—as long as it was a nonviolent method. You were not permitted to hang yourself, shoot yourself, or slash your wrists or other limbs. You could leave the camp and return to the world at any time.

The first camp in Sweden had an occupancy of 250 people. It was filled to capacity from the day it opened. It didn't take long for other camps to open in England, the Netherlands, Switzerland, and Germany. Religious opposition—notably from the Roman Catholic Church— kept the camps from traditionally Catholic states such as Italy, Spain, and France. However, hundreds of residents of those countries—of all religions—crossed the virtually nonexistent borders of western Europe to check in to the Kevorkian camps.

In the United States, the camps opened in Michigan, Maine, Idaho, all across California, and in Arizona. Florida, with a vast elderly population, was one of the first states to outlaw the camps—even before any were proposed in the US.

The camp in Idaho, however, caught the attention of evangelical Christian broadcasters who, having lost the battle over abortion twenty years earlier, now jumped on the Kevorkian camps as obvious examples of Satan at work in America. Instead of referring to them as Kevorkian camps, the preachers brought up memories of the World War II holocaust, calling the retreats "death camps." It was easier to say "death camp" in a headline than say "Kevorkian" or "assisted suicide." The cruel moniker hung over the camps as more and more religious zealots—many of whom had for years insisted that the murder of six million Jews by Nazis in World War II was a hoax—now proclaimed that the Kevorkian camps were in reality secret government concentration camps that were aimed at ridding the country of older citizens.

Entire communities in Florida, Arizona, and the former Mexican states sent mind-boggling contributions of tax dollars to the so-called protectors of older citizens.

There were daily assaults over the airwaves describing in hair-raising detail activities in the camps that never occurred. The self-appointed guardians of the nation's aged vilified Kevorkian, now mouldering in his own grave. They demanded federal, state, local, county, and citizen action to shut down the camps which were called dens of vice, homes of body-snatchers, and the approximation of hell on Earth.

When some of the people who were dying, especially younger people who suffered from incurable wasting diseases, signed wills donating organs to transplant repositories, the anti-Kevorkians wailed that the infirm were being coerced into killing themselves. They unearthed the 1970s film *Soylent Green*—it was shown on some religious television channel (among hundreds) at least once every day—which prophesied suicide as a way of population control and suggested that the proprietors of the Kevorkian camps were making incredible money from the unfortunate and then were turning their bodies into cattle feed—a bizarre offshoot of the movie plot in which the suicide victims became human food.

The claims were believed despite attempts by the Kevorkian camps to carefully document how every penny was spent in the camps and who donated to the camps and how much. For anyone with the stomach to view it, the Kevorkians gave tours of their cremation facilities and how the ashes of the people who committed suicide were either given to relatives in practical urns or were buried on the spacious grounds.

The explanations were ignored. Instead the opponents—claiming that only God and medical science had the right to end life—conjured up fanciful reports of lewd and lascivious conduct in the camps. Orgies among the dead and dying were described daily by "friends" who were shocked at the treatment; other "friends" or "relatives" reported how they saw loved ones left alone to scream in agony for hours until they agreed to kill themselves. "Witnesses" claimed to have seen administrators of the camps move through the barracks late at night and carry away the sick whether they were willing to die or not—and sometimes the friends and relatives who protested went to their fate with them.

Virtually every week, the police departments around the rustic Salmon River camp were forced by signed complaints to go investigate the reported murder of another person. The police dutifully investigated the exaggerated reports and quickly came to realize that contrary to what was being reported from soundproof broadcasting booths and altars of churches, the camps— at least the one in Idaho—were visions of compassion, joy, humane treatment, and an almost God-like way to end one's life.

The rhetoric of the mob of hatemongers, aided by the well-meaning medical profession that bemoaned the death of the patients and predicted that a new treatment to turn the corner on a disease could occur any hour, and certain church edicts—again the Roman Catholic Church being at the forefront—created a mindset that could only lead to disaster.

One evangelist decided to lead a protest to the gates of the Salmon River camp where more than five hundred people and their guests were making their final plans to leave the earth in peace. The evangelist began his crusade in Alabama and marchers along the roads gathered funds and more and more anti-Kevorkians assembled in the giant march across the country. At one point the mass of protesters grew to more than ten thousand and covered three miles along an interstate highway. It was estimated that five thousand people reached the gates of the Salmon River camp.

The Kevorkian Riot was the first and the last of the assaults on the camps. The unruliness of the mob, the televised documentation of the first shot being fired at the police, the attack against authority, and the horrendous assaults recorded against a few of the patients at the Kevorkian camp turned the nation against the anti-Kevorkians.

Most Americans were aware of the camps but hadn't paid a great deal of attention to them unless they had a relative that was dying or was interested in the camps. With the attack on the camp, interest in the camps rose. News crews took their notebooks and their cameras into the camps. The administrators let the crews go by themselves, allowing anyone who didn't mind to be filmed as they lived in the camps—and as they died.

The impact was immediate and far-reaching. By 2040, virtually all the anti-Kevorkian legislation that had been on the books in several states was repealed. The camps now spread everywhere in the country, although areas around Boston and Chicago where there were strong religious commitments against suicide didn't have camps for another decade.

"The will to live is one of the strongest emotions a human being has," the Guide told me. "Men will cut off their arms to keep from being dragged to their death or will slice off their foot if trapped. People will crawl miles to save themselves when horribly injured in an accident.

"But we also know that there is a will to die, too. The will to die has to overcome man's intense will to live. In order for the Kevorkian camps to succeed, the will to die has to be stronger than even the will to live.

"The argument that death is something that should only be left to God is rendered faulty by the fact that many men have shown they have a powerful will to die. The human spirit is too strong to accept that it will be slowly broken through pain and weakness. For some the human spirit embodies the ability to know when it is time to depart and the courage to not only accept that but to reach out and embrace it. It's a fact that we all will discover at one point, but only an individual knows when his time is near. And it's proper that an individual should know it. And be permitted to do something about it as well."

13

Quakes, Floods, and Fires

THE DREAM WOULDN'T GO AWAY. EVEN THOUGH I WAS fully awake—or so I believed—I could still see the faces of anguish and horror on the men and women of some mountain village. They were wailing in some tongue that was unknown to me. I watched as their village collapsed in front of my eyes. Their garments reminded me of the Middle East. My mental television was broadcasting this event, but from where—Afghanistan? Maybe Iran or Turkey.

I could tell I was viewing an earthquake. I've had precognitive dreams like this before. But I was confused: Was this a prediction for today, for next week, for next year? Or was this in some way connected to the trip to Auriesville? Was this part of that vision?

The pitiful, tearful women seemed dazed as they poked through rubble or raised their arms in futile attempts to fend off stones and roofing material.

I got up from bed, instinctively checking the clock—2:57 AM—and groped for the light switch. The incandescent bulb in the lamp at the side of the bed was only twenty-five watts but the light burned through the scene of destruction that faded from my eyes. I walked over to my desk, and began fumbling through the notebook where I had done all the automatic writing weeks before.

I flipped over one page after another, but nothing I saw in the notebook seemed to connect to the dream. I had gone through half the book when a strong masculine voice that arose from inside my head said, "Go back a page. You missed it."

There sitting on the edge of my bed was the Guide. My eyes darted around the room for my bathrobe. "Give me a break," he said. Then he tilted his head and asked, "Correct idiom?" I laughed out loud. "Yes," I told him. "I'm a little amused that you are worried about being idiomatically correct for the time period."

He got up and glided to the desk and peered over my shoulder as the pages of the notebook eerily flipped backwards. "You never should stop learning about people and their times. Stop right there. Knowledge is the greatest gift of the gods and even we who are allegedly immortal must continue to educate ourselves. See what you have written."

Amidst the scrawls and words and drawings, I could make out references to the earth, movement, and destruction.

"But is that the earthquake of the vision of Auriesville or something that is happening right now?" I asked.

"What difference does it make?" the Guide asked rhetorically. "This is one of those things that we cannot predict—if we were exactly right in predicting it there would be worse tragedy than if we didn't tell anyone. Thousands of people would show up to be a part of or a witness to disaster. We should not even be wasting our time on this."

"We've had this argument before," I reminded the Guide. "If I see this terrible event coming, I must warn people about it. Maybe someone will heed the warnings. If I even save one person it's worth it. And if I wasn't supposed to tell anyone, why did I receive the vision in the first place?"

He returned to the bed and sat down. He shrugged.

"Armenia," the Guide said. "That's where the quake that you are seeing will occur. Probably around 2007." And then he explained why this would be an earthquake that would be well remembered, not because of its strength—it was a powerful trembler, around 6.9 on the Richter scale—but because of what happened afterward.

"We idolize those who in the worst of times are at their best. Here in the worst of times, people will act even worse," he said.

It will be a particularly ugly earthquake because while the local government is coping with rescuing hundreds of people trapped in villages and small towns—it won't hit a major metropolitan area—Armenia will be attacked by troops from Azerbaijan. The battle will rekindle long-standing animosities that were especially apparent after the breakup of the Soviet Union. Numerous ceasefires between the warring factions will occur throughout the twenty-first century. Volunteer third parties who rush to help the earthquake victims will get caught up in the ethnic battles. The deaths of several Westerners when a relief truck of supplies is attacked will lead to a lessening of outside assistance to the earthquake victims but won't result in any lessening of tensions and conflicts between the Armenians and the Azerbaijanis.

The murderous attacks included artillery and air assaults on hospitals and makeshift relief operations and overrunning villages that were temporarily cut off due to the earthquake in which inhabitants were raped and butchered by Azerbaijani troops. Outraged Armenians retaliated by repeating the atrocities in Azerbaijani outposts. The earthquake will be over-shadowed by the aftermath to the natural disaster. As usual, human disasters will prove to be far worse than what nature throws at us.

The Guide rubbed his eyes with his left hand as if he was trying to remove the Armenia horror from his memory. "You know," he said, "earthquakes and other natural disasters occur like the weather. And like the weather and horse races, the signs were always there—we just misread them. During the 1970s, researchers were able to come up with so much data and computers with so much number-crunching ability that they could predict—with 100 percent accuracy—the weather twenty-four hours from now. The only hangup was that it took the computers thirty-six hours to process all the information.

"That's the situation here. You've been shown how floods will devastate the planet; how wildfires will cause incredible destruction"—he pointed to another comment in my notebook—"how earthquakes will scar the world. But any small change, the decision to build or not to build a dam, or to approve or disallow a subdivision in a flood zone or on a fire-prone hillside could make some of these predictions moot."

I'd heard the arguments, but I wasn't having any of it. "If we tell the people and they do something about it, it will suffice. If we don't tell anyone about it, and it occurs, I will have been responsible," I told him. "Please, just help me."

The Guide reached out and I beheld a magnificent tableau of what appeared as a great wilderness. No, as we moved in closer, I could make out roads and towns and vehicles on the roads. I could see smoke from campfires. Closer and closer to the ground we progressed, as if we were looking at the world through a zoom lens camera.

"That's Long Lake, New York. It's 2014. Watch," he commanded.

I shuddered as a bridge across the southern end of the lake fell apart and dropped into the water. Each of the scores of wood frame buildings along the highway seemed to implode—they just collapsed in on themselves. The lake seemed to climb out of its basin like some comic book water monster that dashed itself against the ruins of the town.

I was looking at an 8.2 Richter scale earthquake—in the Adirondack Mountains of upstate New York! Earthquakes in New York state? I was astounded by the awful scene of destruction—the village was obliterated—as much as I was by the concept that the area was earthquake prone.

"You Americans of the twentieth century," the Guide scoffed. "You have read so many books predicting that the Big One is something that can only happen in California—and it will—that you forget that the US is a huge country and there are plenty of earthquake faults that are still active."

Some of the most powerful and most devastating earthquakes, the Guide said, occurred in places far from California. The biggest of them all might have been in colonial Connecticut—that gigantic quake in the early 1600s caused such disruptions that even today you can hear the aftershocks in Moodus, Connecticut. In the nineteenth century, earthquakes in New Madrid, Missouri, were powerful enough to change the course of the Mississippi River and sent shock waves strong enough to ring bells in the church steeples in Boston. And if you are talking about earthquakes, the people of Charleston, South Carolina, will remember the devastating shaker in 1886 that nearly destroyed that city.

But since the 1906 earthquake in San Francisco, Californians think they have the patent on violent earthquakes. "Californians should be careful what they wish for. They should especially be concerned in the year 2018," the Guide said as he transformed the view from upstate, pristine New York to the smoggy reaches of Southern California. We looked at a nighttime picture of the Los Angeles basin. He held out his arm and with his finger pointed out the sights as if we were hanging from a hot-air balloon. Los Angeles's avenues and lights spread all the way to the Pacific; far to the south he pointed out San Diego and Tijuana joined by a sea of lights; to the east he pinpointed Riverside, straddling a nearly dry river bed, and nearby, the city of San Bernardino.

Above San Bernardino hung the San Gabriel mountains and scenic Big Bear Lake and scores of small communities. As we watched, Big Bear Lake suddenly lurched. Picture a huge bathtub that is abruptly tilted, with the contents of the lake spilling out. Millions of tons of water rushed down the sides of the mountains, scouring roads and towns into oblivion. Below the onrushing wave of water, the million people of San Bernardino and Riverside were struggling to gain their balance as the 7.7 scale quake jolted them out of bed in the middle of the night. Home after home after home collapsed; fires began to rage as natural gas pipelines ruptured and sparks set off geysers of fire; fires broke out in the street as gasoline station storage tanks failed—some of the gasoline flooded sewers and the ensuing fires raged under the city, punctuated by massive explosions. Streets literally melted. Where the fires failed to turn the streets into a boiling quagmire of hot asphalt, the rumbling earthquake caused yards-wide fissures that made the roads impassable. Highway overpasses collapsed, trapping cars on elevated roadways and blocking access roads below.

The populace barely had time to register the shock of the quake when the torrent from Big Bear swept over them. The water and debris swept around and through the city and having wreaked havoc in San Bernardino, the fury of the water swept along the river channel and crashed into Riverside. The massive waters ignored the channel as if it were just another obstruction, crushing culverts and spilling across homes and businesses with a ferocity that had to be witnessed to be believed. The quake killed thousands in San Bernardino, Riverside, and surrounding communities—deaths were even recorded in Los Angeles where some older buildings collapsed. Poorer and older parts of the cities were wiped out, making exact records of the number of deaths difficult to estimate. But by all estimates, the number of people killed exceeded one hundred thousand, making it the worst natural disaster in the history of the United States.

"The amazing thing about this, of course, is that within five years everything was back to the way it was before 2018," the Guide said.

Survivors who lost everything—family, possessions, pets—used their insurance funds to rebuild. Businesses that disappeared during the dual strikes of earthquake and flood rebuilt in exactly the same spots—"Business was good there," was a remark by a supermarket executive who put up even a bigger store on the spot where the first was destroyed.

"Californians are, er, mind-boggling," the Guide said looking to me for affirmation that he was again idiomatically correct. I simply indicated that he should continue. "Year after year another natural disaster befalls the people. Fires race up arid canyons and destroy million-dollar homes. And before the embers die, new construction is under way even though the likelihood of another horrendous firestorm occurring is great.

"Earthquakes level homes and cause immeasurable damage and heartache. The first act is to build again. The resilience of these people is to be admired even though it is obvious that they have more guts than brains. How good does a view have to be to make someone want to live where they can be knocked out of bed by an earthquake that can be fatal in an instant? Scenery just isn't that important to quality of life."

I pointed to another line in my notebook. This I could tell dealt with a storm. When I would attempt to make reason of the writings I could see massive destruction, wild winds, and huge waves. I realized that I was looking at a hurricane or some other mighty storm, but the details eluded me.

The Guide asked me, "If you were told that there would be such a giant hurricanelike storm and it would cause hundreds of thousands of deaths, where would you expect it to occur?"

"India . . . Bangladesh, perhaps?" I answered.

"Well, of course, Bangladesh. What a sorry place to put a nation. Storms of the century plow ashore in Bangladesh with startling frequency. Even in your own lifetime there have been three deadly storms there since 1970. The twenty-first century won't be any different—only more deadly."

Bangladesh, a country the size of Wisconsin, but inhabited by more than one hundred million people, lies at the head of the Bay of Bengal. The Indian Ocean heats up during the summer and creates cyclones of huge size. In the Indian Ocean the storms are called cyclones; in the Pacific they are typhoons; in the Atlantic they are hurricanes. They are all the same in that they are massive storms that bring death and destruction to huge areas.

In 2013, the first of six major cyclones will roll across Bangladesh. The 2013 storm will come ashore in the Sundarbans, the natural wetlands that are not well populated. The winds of 135 miles per hour will push a storm surge of twenty feet that will inundate the vegetation-covered islands. The dikes protecting many of the small towns and villages in the Sundarbans will collapse from the combined onslaught of wind, rain, and storm surge. Entire villages will be washed away—killing every man, woman, child, goat, cattle, and water buffalo. The storm will howl through the Sundarbans until it plays itself out miles inland. The major city of Khulna will be hard hit. The death toll will exceed fifty thousand, and all of Bangladesh will thank Allah for sparing the country and keeping the death toll so low.

The next storm of the century to strike Bangladesh will occur just eighteen months later. This storm, with sustained winds in excess of 140 miles per hour, will come ashore further west, along the border of Bangladesh and India. Havoc and destruction in Bangladesh will be considerably less this time, with most of the property damage inflicted on Indian territory. The death toll will be under ten thousand, with most of those people dying due to flooding in Calcutta as a result of the deluge brought with the storm. The relatively low loss of life for an India subcontinent cyclone will result in the storm being virtually ignored by the world's media.

Bangladesh will have a twenty-year lull in devastating storms until the cyclone of 2037. That will be the first storm that scientists attempt to defeat while it is still in the ocean by using undersea nuclear explosions to heat water behind the cyclone in an attempt to influence the direction of the storm. The experiments will only kill off massive numbers of fish and create a minor tidal wave that destroys considerable property on the Andaman Islands in the Bay of Bengal.

The attempt to fool Mother Nature fails to alter the course of the killer cyclone, with winds in excess of 170 miles per hour, from slashing up the vulnerable Noakhali District of Bangladesh. The storm, pushing a surge of thirty-five feet over islands where the highest point is ten feet, follows the Bangladesh river system right into the nation's capital of Dhaka. Although the wind speed is slightly diminished—down to 150 miles per hour—and the storm surge accompanying the cyclone is now just twenty feet high, the combination crushes the city of seven million people, taking out government offices, communications, and leaving the nation out of touch with the rest of the world for weeks.

Airports are under water and roads are impassable. Rivers and streams, traditionally the most common form of travel in Bangladesh, are unusable too—because they are covered with debris and the carcasses of humans and animals. The toll in human life is never able to be figured accurately. But no one argues with estimates ranging from two million to four million people dead in the storm. Records are gone, entire cities vanished under the waves. The entire fabric of the country is torn apart. Ironically, Bangladesh, one of the nations that most frequently sent its troops to be part of United Nations' peacekeeping operations, now finds itself under United Nations "protection."

United Nations forces are to be in Bangladesh only until the conclusion of the emergency. The original estimates are that it will take at least fifteen years to rebuild the nation's basic infrastructure, reestablish a government civil service, and hold free and fair elections.

The role of the UN in Bangladesh is hampered by other onslaughts of nature—in 2050, 2052, and 2074. None of these storms comes close to being as devastating as the storm of 2037, but as each storm strikes—testing UN storm protection projects to protect many communities—new setbacks to the UN timetable occur.

A limited UN presence—which means that complete self-government has not been reestablished—will remain in effect until the end of the twenty-first century.

"Shawn, you are right about the field of blue in your vision. The UN flag will fly over every continent by the end of the twenty-first century, and in very few places will the inhabitants of UN-governed territory be happy about it.

"Even in Bangladesh, which through UN tutelage will begin to see a decent level of prosperity reach even the lowest economic levels of its huge population, there will still be a majority that would rather rule themselves in poverty than be ruled by someone else and prosper.

"Having food in the belly—even in Bangladesh— doesn't cure the hunger for freedom and self-determination."

14

UKRAINE AXIS

IF YOU LIVE IN DES MOINES OR BOISE OR EVEN Nashville, the daily routine in my neighborhood in Greenwich Village would seem bizarre. About 7 AM people begin spilling out of their homes and, depending on the weather, walk or dash to their cars, turn on the ignition, and quickly drive the vehicles across the street, they then hop out of the cars and return to their homes. Ah, the joys of alternate side of the street parking.

This morning, instead of trotting out to the car in a raincoat with my bathrobe on underneath, I had actually taken the time to put on some slacks and a blouse and, after completing the alternate side of the street tradition, I walked down to the coffee shop/deli on the corner where I treated myself to a Danish, downed a couple of cups of coffee, and devoured the *Times*, the *Post*, and the *Daily News*. I convinced myself that I needed a break from my notes and the anxieties that the interpretation of the visions were causing.

I'd just completed this task and was returning to my apartment—which I had carefully locked up tighter than a drum. As I unlocked the door, I distinctly heard voices, the kind of voices you hear on the television. I was concerned because 1) I was so caught up in trying to decipher the visions that I'd forgotten I'd turned the set on before I left the house; 2) I thought a burglar had seen me leave and had managed to get into the apartment in the time I was gone and was now watching television while he leisurely robbed the place; or 3) I'd forgotten that someone was staying with me.

The answer, of course, was 4) none of the above. Relaxing in my sofa, watching *The Bridge Over the River Kwai*, was the Guide. "I love this movie," he said as the credits began to roll. "Remember the ending, the officer screaming, 'Madness! Madness! Madness!' It's prophetic. 'When will they ever learn?' as Peter, Paul, and Mary sing. The answer, Shawn, isn't blowing in the wind; the answer is, they are just too stupid to learn. It is all madness. Sometimes I wonder if it's worth doing what we are doing? I wonder if anyone will ever pay attention? How many warnings can we give before someone does something?"

I stared at the Guide. "A depressed ghost?" I said. "Who would have guessed?" He gave me a withering look.

"By the way," I asked, "how did you turn on the television set?"

"I can transport you to a different time and place in an instant, something you accept without question, and you wonder how I can turn on a TV set? Just remember that I can do it, that's all you really need to know."

The television emitted a short *pop* and the screen went blank. "Okay, Shawn, let's get back to work."

I was going to ask where we were going to start when the notebook with my writings floated to me, worked its way into my hand. Somehow my thumb moved down the page and stopped. "Danger." "Axis." "Popular tyranny." Those were the words I read. I'd looked at them before and realized they all had to do with the same thing because they were intertwined in the scrawl. I had also written some Cyrillic lettering—

a friend whose ancestors were Russian had told me that—so I had an inkling that we were talking about a happening in Russia. But when I had gone into the strobe-light-induced trance, the images had no meaning to me. I could see armies and weapons and saw images that reflected dangerous conflicts, but nothing fit into place. For the umpteenth time I had been frustrated by what I was seeing and not knowing what it was that was taking place.

Now as I looked at my notes I observed the floor of the apartment become transparent and then disappear. Below me I could see the earth as a giant globe. But I knew what I was seeing wasn't real. When you look at the earth from space, you can differentiate between oceans and continents, between lakes and mountains, but you can't tell where one country ends and another begins (except for the border between Haiti and the Dominican Republic—the Haitian half of the island of Hispaniola is denuded of vegetation. The border looks almost as if a line was drawn on the land).

But on this globe, all the countries were clearly marked. The political boundaries were clear. The globe turned until I was looking at the Eurasian continent. The massive body of Russia was clearly visible. I knew France and England and Germany and Italy. But, I confess, what I know about European geography would be the smallest book ever printed.

"This really isn't my strong suit," I said to the Guide, appealing for help with my cast-down eyes.

He began to give me a lesson in geopolitics and the more I learned the more I feared. And the more I knew why the Guide was whistling Peter, Paul, and Mary tunes.

"Hatred," he said, "is an emotion that will overcome all rational thought. All lessons of history are lost when you teach your youth, your young, and your neighbors how to hate."

The roots of conflict in eastern Europe are all based on deep-seated distrust and the historical power of Russia as the dominant force in Eastern Europe. It was the Russians who subjected the Ukrainians and White Russians over generations; the Russians as Soviets who enslaved the Warsaw Pact nations and grabbed huge chunks of territory in Poland and Romania. Poles were therefore mistrustful of Russia and fearful of Germany. Fifty years of relative peace had done little to alleviate the animosities that lingered in the hearts of children and grandchildren of the oppressed. The chaos that reigns in what used to be Yugoslavia is a tragic case in point.

Early in the twenty-first century it became apparent to all nations around the world that democracy would hold sway over Russia even if the huge population was determined to make a mess of governing itself. The powerful Red Army, a force which could have easily taken over the country at a moment's notice any time during and after the coups of the 1990s, remained in the barracks—dedicated only to saving Mother Russia from attacks from external enemies.

Internally, the Red Army watched with bemusement as the nation moved in fits and starts to elect one leader, depose him in another hastily called election, and then recall the original 'villain' in an overwhelming victory only to oust him the next time the country voted.

The attempts to throw off seventy years of communism with a free market economy similarly moved forward on bumpy seas. Political wags were constantly making comparisons between Russia and pre–World War II France or post-World War II Italy. They wondered why a country such as Russia would pick up the habits of the most incompetent of democracies.

Fortunately for the Russians, the nations with the most at stake in seeing democracy thrive in the Russian behemoth—the United States and Japan—helped financially to pull Russia over some of the major obstacles in her path to successful self-determination. Much to the chagrin of the US and Japan, Russia's pre-communist era traditional allies—namely France—turned a cold shoulder to Russia, letting the nation of 250 million stumble through most of the first quarter of the twenty-first century.

About 2015, something sinister emerged in Central Europe. As Western Europe gained in prosperity due to the success of the European Community that tore down regional borders and tariffs, Central Europe became concerned that that region was being cut out of the pie.

Led by nationalist fervor, the Ukraine—the breadbasket of Europe—forged a series of new agreements that created a new power on the continent. The Ukraine, Belarus—also known as White Russia—and the Baltic states of Latvia, Lithuania, and Estonia agreed to major economic and military pacts that at one stroke created a powerful armed force on the continent. The five states, led by virtual one-party leadership, unearthed the oldest and foulest demagoguery to capture the jingoistic hearts of their countrymen. Russians were vilified as blood-letting invaders; Jews were again reviled as the architects of financial ruin; Poles were dismissed as subhumans; foreigners who were helping to rebuild small business were attacked by fascist gangs. There was no mistaking the types of attacks. The Ukraine and its allies were tied by economic, geographic, nationalistic, and racist links. The rest of the world watched with worry and fear.

The Ukraine never surrendered its nuclear weapons after the breakup of the Soviet Union, contending that as long as Russia had nuclear bombs and as long as Germany, through NATO, had such weapons, the Ukraine needed the weapons, too.

The Central Axis, as the group of five soon became known—conjuring up the evil connotations of the German-Italian-Japanese axis of World War II—controlled the center of the continents, from the Baltic

Sea to the Black Sea. It had as its main resource the ability to supply food to virtually the entire world, now that the governments of Ukraine and Belarus had allowed western agriculture experts to show how to properly farm the vast, fertile plains of central Europe. On the pretext of needing troops to protect its borders against the unstable Russia and the weak buffer states of the former Warsaw Pact, the Central Axis raised a huge army that was well-equipped and anxious to show how strong it was.

In 2020, the leadership of Belarus and Lithuania started rattling sabers and casting an imperialistic eye towards the isolated Kaliningrad Oblast, an artifact of World War II.

At the end of World War I, the nation of Poland was created where no nation previously existed. In creating Poland, the settlement imposed on Germany split Germany into two sections. The Polish Corridor—which became a battleground in World War II—separated East Prussia from Germany. East Prussia's capital was the important port city of Koenigsberg.

Following the disastrous World War II, the borders of Europe changed markedly. All of East Prussia was taken from Germany. The southern half of the province became Polish territory, partially to compensate Poland for having half its territory taken over by the Soviet Union. The new Polish state included much of East Prussia and considerable chunks of eastern Germany. The land that used to be Poland until Stalin joined Hitler in dividing Poland in 1939 became part of the Ukraine or Belarus. The rest of East Prussia, including Koenigsberg, was ceded to the Soviet Union and the name of Koenigsberg was changed to Kaliningrad. The name of the entire Soviet province that was the former East Prussia was called the Kaliningrad Oblast, and was part of the Russian Federated Soviet Socialist Republic. It mattered little at the time that Kaliningrad was separated from Russia by three hundred miles of Lithuania and White Russia (also known as Byelorussia and later as independent Belarus) because the political reality was that Lithuania and White Russia were all part of the single government of the Soviet Union.

It became a problem in 1992 when the Soviet Union disintegrated into more than a dozen independent states. Now this little piece of Russia was cut off from Moscow. Issues of sovereignty aside, Kaliningrad was important to Moscow because it represented Russia's only port on the Baltic Sea—and during winter, Russia's only ice-free port to the west.

The problem of Kaliningrad soon took center stage in the political theater of Europe. The territory soon became coveted once it became obvious that Russia was in no condition to successfully defend the territory. Poland on the south desired to take over the territory to complete the occupation of East Prussia; Lithuania cited historical and geographic reasons that it should take control of certain peninsulas and islands that surrounded the oblast's important harbor. Belarus chimed in on the side of Lithuania—the latter nation guaranteeing Belarus use of the port if Lithuania gained control of the territory. If Belarus had free access to the port, then the White Russians would finally have direct access to the sea. Russia cited history, eighty years of the status quo, and the fact that it had a lot of troops already in place as enough reason to maintain for the other states to back off.

But the expansion-minded Central Axis—joined in 2022 by Moldova in the south, and now allied with Romania and Slovakia and having signed a nonaggression treaty with Poland—moved serious numbers of troops to the Kaliningrad borders. In concert, Poland marched a division of infantry along the southern border of Kaliningrad; Lithuanian gunships began operating in international waters outside the port of Koenigsberg. The fate of Kaliningrad seemed sealed—it was going to be devoured by the Central Axis and Poland. In fact, secret meetings between the nations involved had already determined who would get what when the order was given for troops to march. Russia yelled and screamed and threatened to use force itself to protect Kaliningrad, but no one took the threats seriously. There was no way that Russia could supply Kaliningrad—unless it overran parts of Finland and no one could see that scenario being acted out.

In a last-minute appeal—attempts to get the conflict mediated by the United Nations failed because Russia vetoed suggestions that the Russian territory be carved up by plebiscite—Russia asked NATO for assistance. The request—in papers made public in 2092 it was revealed, as most people suspected at the time, that Germany actually told Russia to make the request—was put on the table for discussion by NATO at the same time that Central Axis and Polish forces moved across the borders of Kaliningrad. Russian troops put up stiff resistance although it was a foregone conclusion that the Russian forces would be unable to hold back the superior numbers of troops.

Not waiting for a decision by NATO, the German parliament—aware of the strong ties to East Prussia ("We must aid our German brothers," members of the German parliament cried, despite the fact that the number of people who were once German and still lived in Kaliningrad could be counted on one hand)—authorized the German military to "assist" Russian troops in "maintaining order" in Kaliningrad. Faced with the prospect of battling well-trained, well-supplied, and much-feared Germans, as opposed to well-trained, under-supplied, and wishy-washy Russians, the Polish–Central Axis advance ground to a halt. The United States, England, and France were appalled at the Germans' unilateral move, but after hemming and hawing they reluctantly backed their NATO ally's position. Thousands of NATO troops, ships, and aircraft were protecting the piece of territory while diplomats tried their hand at unraveling the mess.

Everyone held their positions and waited. The negotiations dragged out for more than fifteen years, before Russia gave in and accepted the idea of a plebiscite so the people of Kaliningrad could choose their own fate. The citizens were given a series of questions: unilateral independence, union with Lithuania—certain parts, union with Poland, continued political union with Russia. The last was demanded by Russia for her approval to hold the plebiscite. Germany had attempted to get a question of union with Germany on the ballot, but it never got past the trial balloon stage.

The results dumbfounded the experts and created the political stalemate that afflicted central Europe for the rest of the twenty-first century. The people of Kaliningrad decided they wanted to remain part of Mother Russia. And they wanted NATO forces to continue to stay in their country.

The upshot of the tension around Kaliningrad was that the war machinery of Europe that politicians at the start of the twenty-first century were sure could be ground into plowshares was instead draining all European economies. NATO assessed its membership for additional troops and supplies; the Central Axis converted civilian factories that were turning out personal automobiles into factories manufacturing tanks and military transports; Russia, so hopeful of concentrating on its economy, again found major portions of its budget funneled into supplies for the huge Red Army. The growth of Europe as the economic wonder of the twenty-first century was stillborn by what most analysts considered a rather insignificant piece of land. But with national honor and ethnic honor at stake, the Kaliningrad crucible boiled throughout the century.

"Hate was the victor in Central Europe," the Guide muttered. "Ukrainians hate the Russians because they have never forgiven Stalin and the communists for subjecting their nation after World War I and then killing millions during the force famines of the 1930s. The White Russians have yearned for freedom since the

Russian Revolution of 1917 and looked again at Russia as an imperialist that cannot be trusted. The Baltics sent many of their young to die on the barricades in attempts to overthrow Moscow," the Guide recounted. "There was too much hatred to ever ally with Moscow, so instead they allied their hatred to create the conditions for more chaos and death in the world.

"The Central Axis didn't learn in the twenty-first century the lessons of the twentieth century. You may ask, how many years will it take till they know that too many people have died."

The Guide shook his head. "Don't look at me. I don't have the answer." He rifled through the notebook of my writings. "And the answer isn't in here either." He pointed down at the globe, still turning slowly at our feet. The continent of Europe now turned a liquid red, with color oozing into the Black Sea and across the borders of the countries.

"Maybe, maybe, someone down there," he said, pointing to the continent, "will have an answer before the entire continent bleeds into the seas."

15

SOUTH AFRICA

THE MICROWAVE OVEN HUMMED PLEASANTLY, DUTI-fully zapping a frozen dinner into a state of passing palatability. Out of the corner of my eye, I thought I saw movement—perhaps a figure—in the living room. My first thought was that it must be the Guide, making another of his drop-in visits. And, of course, the New Yorker in me also considered, "Or it could be the burglar-robber-rapist the tabloids are clamoring about."

I weighed my choices and decided to wait out dinner. If it was a burglar, I figured I could offer him dinner and see if he was poisoned.

The microwave pinged, and I gingerly turned the maca-roni and cheese out from its semi-cardboard container onto a plate. I ate silently for a couple of minutes, but finally my curiosity got the better of me. I carried the plate into the living room, and there, at my desk and working under the lamp was the Guide, peering intently over a large magnifying glass.

I put the plate down on the sofa end table and walked up to the Guide. I could see the magnifying glass but I couldn't make out what he was looking at.

"Here," he said, reading my thoughts as usual, "see for yourself."

I picked up the lens, turned it over in my hand, and then looked at the table again. All I could see was the fine patina. He pointed to a certain spot. I placed the glass over the spot and leaned over.

I seemed to be falling into a great chasm. I was looking down a long tube that seemed to be a mile away. A feeling of dizziness and nausea overcame me. I hate flying in planes because whenever I look out the window at the ground, I can feel my stomach turn. A moment of panic overcame me. For an instant I didn't know where I was and now I wasn't even sure when I was. I jerked my head away from the lens. I was back in my apartment.

The Guide smirked and motioned back to the table. I picked up the glass again, sat down in the chair, and slowly moved my eyes to the center of the glass. I was ready for the tube this time. Quickly an object at the end of the tube came closer and swam into focus. It was red and triangle-shaped. It took a couple of seconds to realize that the object was a postage stamp, although unlike any stamp I'd ever seen. It was cut smooth, no perforations were on the sides. It seemed old and somewhat crude in design. It was also postmarked, although I couldn't read the city or the date. It wasn't from the United States. It read "Cape of Good Hope."

I cautiously lifted my head and returned to my home again. I turned a quizzical eyebrow on the Guide. "A postage stamp?" I asked.

"Yes, and no," the Guide said. "It was a postage stamp in the late nineteenth century. In the twenty-first century it was getaway cash."

The map of southern Africa appeared over the wall of my apartment in Greenwich Village and, as if the map were at the end of a camera, the map became larger and more detailed. When the camera stopped, the city of Pretoria stood out at the center. The walls of the apartment faded away, and the Guide began a history lesson that began in 1850 and ended 250 years later.

Despite horrifying massacres between black factions in South Africa the one-time bastion of apartheid became a land of majority rule as the twenty-first century began. But even after blacks gained control of their country's political process, the ethnic, tribal and political violence continued to worsen.

As long as the violence only seemed to affect black groups fighting for political control, the wealthy and influential white population stayed put. But early in the twenty-first century, the violence spilled into the exclusive white settlements. Atrocities that were once perpetrated by official white South Africans upon the majority blacks were now being committed by majority blacks on the minority whites.

Police control of the mobs attacking and killing the whites was less than efficient and the black-controlled court system treated the offenders with far more restraint than the white victims demanded. About 2007 the whites from South Africa were openly fleeing the country. White merchants and ranchers and mansion owners were quietly and quickly turning their assets into cash or jewelry, trying to get as much of their life savings out of South Africa as possible. It wasn't anything new. Restrictions about taking cash from the country had been in place for decades.

To combat the attempt to remove assets from the country, the new government shut down electronic business transfers. Exit points throughout South Africa became hour-long waits as teams of men and women carefully searched every nook and cranny of departing individuals' luggage and bodies for attempts to remove anything of value from the country.

That's when the "Cape Triangles" became the emigrates' item of choice to smuggle. In 1853, the first postage stamps of the Cape of Good Hope were issued. The British Colony issued several stamps in a triangle design. In perfect condition the stamps are worth thousands of dollars—one issued in error in 1861 is worth more than $100,000. The size of the stamps, their value, and the fact that they could be hidden so easily—and then could be rapidly exchanged among the stamp dealers of the world for dollars, yen, or pounds Sterling outside South Africa—made the triangles getaway money for thousands of fleeing whites (and many wealthy blacks who could smell disaster for the country down the road).

By 2028, South Africa was a virtually black country, politically and economically. There were still whites there as teachers and in some technical positions, but their numbers were small and their influence was nil.

And the black-on-black violence that was occurring with terrifying regularity in the 1990s didn't slow at all through the first quarter of the twenty-first century. Elections were fixed by the ruling party, and only violence succeeded in getting a change of government—and then the new government raised corruption to a new standard, until another group was successful in another violent coup.

In 2037, another in the succession of coups bounced the acting government, claiming—truthfully—that the "ins" were woefully inept and shockingly corrupt. The nation's infrastructure was crumbling—the collapse of a gold mine that killed 487 miners in 2036 attesting to worn-out structures and officials who looked the other way when inspecting the mines.

The overthrown government quickly gave up the seats of power, agreeing to abdicate without bloodshed if it was permitted to retain control over a small enclave outside Pretoria. The coup leaders, more interested in making themselves rich than fighting over a small piece of territory, agreed. What the new government didn't know was that their enemy—while in power—had discovered secret plans to build atomic weapons in a manufacturing plant near Pretoria.

In the 1970s, isolated and under guerrilla attack from

its black African neighbors to the north, the white regime in South Africa began to develop a nuclear weapons capability.

The announced theory was to build nuclear devices that would help "mining" operations. In actuality, the government was building an atomic weapon supply that could be dropped from the air to destroy an invading army or the home base of that army. In 1989, the government ordered the destruction of the nuclear weapons and the conversion of the nuclear weapons plant into a facility for peaceful purposes.

The cynics of the time pointed to South Africa's steady movement towards the end of the era of apartheid and said that the reason South Africa's white government was dismantling the bombs was to make sure that no black power on earth had nuclear capability.

But no matter how well you convert a nuclear weapons plant into something else, the possibility of rekindling the weapons programs is frighteningly real. The group in control of the factory recognized in its last grasp of power how important it would be to start the weapons manufacture again—if it later lost control of the government.

"When you've been in and out of power two or three times, it's a simple prediction to figure you'll be overthrown again," the Guide digressed.

When the inevitable occurred in 2037 and they were overthrown, the faction held on to the reconverted plant. Since only the top leaders of the group knew what was there, the new ruling powers ignored the stronghold while getting the rest of the country under their control and setting up a flourishing system of corruption, bribes, and payoffs that made previous governments look like amateurs.

In fact, the new government was so successful in organizing corruption that the country prospered—as long as no one was too concerned about individual rights. The new leaders invited investment from overseas, usually in the form of organized crime figures who set up magnificent resorts and casinos. With some of the best-trained thugs and goons known to mankind, these resorts became the "in" places in the world by 2044.

Meanwhile, the rebels, still holding strong to their secret factory with a couple of hundred thousand faithful (those who had turned on the "ins" previously) continued to plot to retake control of the government. The "official" government was too busy making fortunes from mining and gambling and tourist enterprises to care about the radical group among them. Besides, to eradicate the foes would mean unfavorable publicity.

As more and more Americans and Europeans came to South Africa to gamble and visit awe-inspiring scenic displays, hordes of reporters—many looking for a free vacation in a warm climate—followed the tourists, writing mainly about the resurgence of South Africa as the gem of the continent.

Most of the reporters ignored stories about dissidents who disappeared since the dissidents who approached the reporters usually ended up as lion food on a game preserve.

In 2047, the rebels hijacked a helicopter—actually they bought it from a soldier for $70,000 and then knocked him cold for effect. The soldier claimed he was attacked, but he was turned over to the Chicago crime lord interrogation team and blurted out the truth after five minutes of "discussion." He and his family were sent off to a game preserve.

But the helicopter was now in the hands of the rebels, who loaded it with one of their newly complete nuclear bombs and placed it aboard the chopper. The pilots of the helicopter were told to fly low along the ground and then rise three thousand feet into the air, arm the bomb, and push it off. The selected site was the first and most famous of the casinos built along the eastern coast of the country near Durban. The pilots were assured that they would have plenty of time to get away, which, of course, was a lie.

The bomb was dropped in the middle of the night while the tables were full of raucous, happy, and soon-to-be-dead gamblers. In reality it was a fairly modest bomb, but it still cremated 150,000 people in a fraction of a second—including the unlucky helicopter crew.

The rebels immediately went on pirate radio to announce that they were the ones that had nuked the casino and demanded that the government surrender to them.

However, the rebels made a strategic error. Because they had to steal a helicopter to deliver the first bomb—and that helicopter was now reduced to elements—the government realized that the rebels might have more bombs but had no way to deliver them. The government, aided by the Burson-Marsteller public relations firm, which had officers in every country on earth and two in space, began a vicious campaign against the rebels. Pictures of some of the bodies that were only maimed—not disintegrated—were shown on broadcasts. The entire campaign was to inflame the already outraged citizenry into murderous action. With government troops and transports assisting, more than a million citizens with small arms, machetes, and sticks and pipes attacked the rebel stronghold.

Wave after wave of South Africans rose over the defense barriers and slaughtered anyone living on the other side. They were encouraged to raze the enclave, to kill, rape, mutilate, and destroy anyone loyal to the barbarians who would launch a nuclear attack against their own people.

The orgy of slaughter occurred without the glare of television or videotape—the government was careful to make sure than none of these weapons of public opinion could be turned against them. Tens of thousands of the ill-armed citizens died at the hands of the staunch defenders of the enclave who had automatic weapons. But the enraged (and later revealed, doped up) mob used their fallen comrades' bodies as shields and pressed forward. The automatics ran out of bullets and the defenders were massacred by the hundreds, their heads and limbs tossed around like souvenir pieces of goalposts after a college football game.

The horror and the bloodshed were captured on a few well-concealed still cameras that survived detection as the mob concentrated on killing each other as brutally as possible. Three days of hand-to-hand fighting—with an occasional assist from an assault helicopter—brought the battle to the heavily armed, bunkered factory where other nuclear weapons were stored.

The leaders of the rebel group now faced extinction from the howling, bloodthirsty mob driven even more insane by drugs, heat, and the frenzy of the kill. The leaders realized they were doomed and that their plot to retake the government had completely failed; they realized that there was no hope that they or any of their family or their supporters would receive any clemency or even a decent death. They armed one of the remaining three bombs they had left—the blast would destroy the others—sent out an hour-long harangue on their just cause, and fired the weapon.

The bunker was built strongly enough so that the blast didn't initially destroy a vast area. However, they selected, either on purpose or unwittingly, a most opportune or unfortunate time, depending upon your personal framework, to achieve local Armageddon. A particularly strong wind carried radioactive debris towards the east, eventually causing the deaths of thousands of people living in Pretoria, and making the historic capital of South Africa uninhabitable until 2092.

"Oh God, oh God," I cried as I could see the devastation and death spread out in front of me. "Something must be done to prevent this. Can't we do anything at all?"

The Guide looked as grim as the landscape of the future South Africa. "You are standing on the path that will take us to this scene in fifty years. As long as we stand on this path, that scene you have just witnessed will rush toward us as a runaway train. What you have to do is to get off this path and create another path."

My eyes teared. "Me?" I questioned. "It's up to me to do this? How is that possible? How is that fair, to put such a burden on me?"

"You have the power of the visions. You have to tell what will be. Perhaps someone will listen. Perhaps the one person who can make a difference will hear you. Perhaps he will not. What we do know is where this path leads."

I tried to grasp what he was saying. I wanted to get a better response. But I already could see his features begin to fade. He was moving away from me again to his own time or maybe to another time. Now more than ever I needed guidance from my Guide. And he was gone. Now, I wondered, would he return? Or was his work with me finished, too?

16

RELIGION IN THE 21ST CENTURY

THE GUIDE STOPPED IN FRONT OF EVERY CHURCH HE saw in New York City. He studied the edifices somberly for long periods. As we would approach a church, he and I would talk either psychically or verbally. Then at once the conversation would cease. No thoughts would emanate from him—or at least none were directed at me that I could perceive.

"Religion," he mused one day in front of St. Patrick's Cathedral, "is the defining characteristic of mankind. There is a deep-seated need to believe in all of us; a need to believe that what we are isn't all that we are. We need to know that somehow, somewhere there is someone, something who can ascend above our own frailties of character. Unfortunately, the way we have determined to pursue that uncertain something has caused immeasurable havoc and harm to society."

As he scrutinized the architecture of the church, I shooed away the ever-present New York City official bird, the pigeon, from our feet. I didn't want to see what happened when a gray pigeon pecked at the sandal-clad feet of a ghost. What would happen if a pigeon . . . I giggled at the thought. The Guide wrinkled his forehead in disdain.

"All through your writings are mentions and symbols of religion," he said. I fished into my purse to retrieve my notebook of writings.

Indeed, on almost every page was a cross, a Star of David, the half-crescent moon that represents Islam, and other symbols that I found to represent sects and religions of the Far East and of the tribes of Africa. When I had gone into a trance and tried to focus on these symbols and bring some depth to their meaning, the messages failed to make a lot of sense. The only thing that did reveal itself to me, I thought, was a cross—which in my thoughts represented the Roman Catholic Church—and an austere image of a robe-clad figure whom I could identify by the traditional garments as the pope. The strange part of the image that I was seeing, however, was that this future pope was unmistakably a man of African descent—the first black pope.

"Yes," the Guide said, "you are right. There will be a pope elected in the Roman Catholic Church who will be of African descent. It will become a historic and telling moment in the history of the Roman Catholic Church. But it won't be a pretty picture."

The election of Pope John Paul II in the 1970s changed a part of the history of the church. It ended the stranglehold that Italy had on the election of popes. John Paul II widened the ethnicity of the College of Cardinals, creating the atmosphere of reform in how the church elects the man who is revered as the embodiment of St. Peter.

But Pope John Paul II wasn't the liberal pope that many Catholics, especially those in western Europe and the United States, had hoped would lead the world's billion Catholics. His successors in the late 1990s and early twenty-first century slowly began to loosen the tight reigns the Holy See held over its flock. Celibacy among priests and nuns became optional (although there were still orders that demanded and enforced celibacy); birth control measures were permitted but only after major counseling sessions with parish priests (abortion was still taboo); divorce was allowed as the church recognized that man was imperfect and could not be expected to always achieve God-like perfection in selecting a mate.

Analysts were surprised by the changes in the church—which resulted in a revitalization of the religion in the United States. Parishes that closed around major cities were reconsecrated as the more liberal doctrines of the church sent worshippers back to their pews in droves. Huge numbers of worshippers had left the church years before because they had divorced and they felt shunned by church leaders. These fallen-away Catholics had remarried outside the church and had raised new families, all of whom were estranged from the church. When the reforms—especially the divorce reform—were initiated, these Catholics once again returned to the fold.

One of the major reasons the analysts were surprised by the changes was because the changes came at the hands of the Italian bloc that recaptured the papacy after Pope John Paul II. Some church watchers expressed the blasphemous idea that a deal was struck by the liberal camp of the church to elect an Italian only if the candidate secretly agreed to significant reform. Naturally, the suggestion of a deal—a political payoff—in the election of a pope was scoffed at by spokesmen for the Vatican, but it proved to be a question that never faded away.

A succession of popes were Italian until 2036 when a Spaniard was elected. His reign was brief. His replacement began the Americanization of the Vatican. The first American pope was elected in the chair of St. Peter in 2042, and Americans kept the chair for forty

years, until the election of an American who was also
the first African-American pope in 2082.

The reaction to his election was phenomenal. After
all, America had elected a black president years before
and no one had blinked an eye that that president was
a woman! But the naming of the black pope caused
convulsions deep within many of the ethnically strong
church congregations—such as the Poles, the Italians,
the French Catholics in Quebec. Some Roman Catholic churches simply refused to accept the black pope as
their leader; threats of assassination were made publicly
and regularly (no attempts were ever reported, although
there were several suspected); a new schism developed
in the church, and it wasn't limited to congregations in
the south of the United States. There were metropolitan Catholic Churches that broke away; rural churches
in upstate New York refused to acknowledge the new
pope; the entire archdiocese of Rhode Island considered
starting its own church before emissaries from Rome
used a combination of public cajoling and iron-fisted
backroom politics to keep the archdiocese in line.

"It only had to do with race," the Guide explained.
"Men and women whose own children had married members of other faiths or other races or supported their
children who were in homosexual relationships were
now dead-set against having a black man lead them in
prayer. It was ugly and it was mean spirited. It brought
out the worst of people in even the best of times."

The split in the church was clearly racial in nature.
It was one thing to be led in prayer by a man of a different race at the local parish, but it was something else
again to believe that a black man was the embodiment
of St. Peter. Some of the people who opposed the election of the black pope feared that by saying that the post
of pope was acceptable to a man of color it meant that
perhaps even Jesus was a man of color—a theory that
had lingered for generations. In fact, there was considerable justification both in scripture and in anthropology

to suggest that Jesus might very well have been a person of color: The chance of Jesus being a blond-haired, blue-eyed Caucasian isn't as good as the chance that Jesus was indeed a black man.

The effect of electing a black pope, however, didn't have long-term consequences. The reign was relatively short. When he was elected, the pope already knew that he had been suffering from colon cancer. The disease was thought to be in remission at that time, but in reality, it had spread to other organs. The pope was given powerful courses of chemotherapy and radiation and was offered the opportunity to have multiple organ transplants. But he turned down the heroic procedures. "There are others who can use those organs to live a full life," the pope explained from his hospital bed, where he was undergoing additional chemotherapy. "I am satisfied that I have had the chance to fulfill the spiritual needs of all Catholics, no matter how long that opportunity has existed."

The quiet courage of the pope subdued the opposition to his reign. The protests vanished as the world's Catholics and all people of color followed the pope's downward spiral. In one of his final interviews, given to the official media of the Vatican, the pope allowed that he realized that his color was divisive to the religion, but he prayed that future popes of color wouldn't have to deal with color—only with doctrine.

The black pope sat on the throne of St. Peter for just two years. He was followed by the first man in two thousand years who was born in the Holy Land to be elected pope. The pope from Jerusalem had a dark complexion, but the new pope never addressed any questions as to his race. Since the media couldn't get any answer about his race, they stopped asking the question. It no longer seemed important to anyone. "I represent all mankind and all mankind are my brothers and sisters," the Jerusalem pope stated once early in his long reign. It became his motto and featured a successful—read that noncontroversial—reign that continued into the twenty-second century.

The twenty-first century turned out to be fairly successful for organized Roman Catholicism. Although the religion had ups and downs, it emerged from the twenty-first century far stronger than it was in the mid-twentieth century. Roman Catholics claimed more congregants and more regular churchgoers than any time previously in the church's history. But for the Catholic church's greatest rival of the twenty-first century, Islam, the story was considerably different.

Orthodox Islam entered the twenty-first century seemingly in a position to become a dominant force in the world. There were one hundred million Muslims in Indonesia. The 120 million people of Bangladesh had declared themselves an Islamic Republic, and there were movements around the world to create more and more countries that would be ruled by the word of the Koran. Muslim fundamentalists seemed to be on the rise near the end of the twentieth century, with powerful, ambitious, and dangerous elements and movements at work in Egypt, Iraq, and sub-Saharan states such as Nigeria, Mauritania, and Mali. The possibility of gaining stronger ground in the former Soviet states of Kazakhstan, Turkmenistan, and Uzbekistan—all with huge Muslim populations—led some political commentators to assume that Islam was the religion on the move.

It just didn't work out that way.

Kazakhstan, the territory the size of Texas that borders Iran and Afghanistan on the south and Russia on the north, was seen as a barometer of how far Islam would succeed among the Muslim-dominated former Soviet states. But as early as 2005 it became apparent that the leadership of Kazakhstan was more interested in developing the rich potential resources of the country than allowing its religious community to dictate the path through the twenty-first century.

Kazakhstan beckoned to the West and offered terrific business deals to Europeans and Americans who were seeking new capitalistic markets to sell goods and remove minerals from the land. The Kazakhs knew that vast parts of their country contained arid, near-desert territory. The Kazakhs jumped on the "Peace in the Holy Land" bandwagon and used improving relations between Israel and its Arab neighbors to extend an invitation to Israeli hydrologists to come to Kazakhstan and come up with ways of turning near desert into fields of green—similar to what Israel had accomplished at home.

Instead of becoming a leader of Islam, Kazakhstan became a leader in bringing the predominantly Islamic country to the forefront as an economic colossus. The nation prospered in industry and in agriculture, the per capita income rose, schools flourished. Impressively, as the country grew stronger economically and democratically, so did Islam. The numbers of devout Muslims in Kazakhstan grew and so did their fervor. Yet the idea of converting the democratic nation to a religious state in the mode of other Islamic republics never developed. Under the Kazakhstan constitution all religions were treated equally—even though 75 percent of the population considered itself Muslim—and, more importantly, religion was separated from the state.

With the example of Kazakhstan shining through, the other Islamic-majority former Soviet states adopted similar governments and policies. They too prospered—more than Mother Russia, but less than Kazakhstan. The ability of these newest states to balance religion and democracy and economics took the wind out of the sails of the fundamentalist movements in the former Soviet states and also weakened movements around the world for the creation of more Islamic republics in other Moslem-majority states. In sub-Saharan Africa, these states were too busy coping with the multiple disasters of famine, drought, and AIDS to get involved in assisting other movements—especially the guerrilla campaign in Egypt.

The struggle in Egypt between the forces of democracy—although not a true multiparty state for much of the twenty-first century—and the forces of orthodox religion was ugly and bloody. Numerous attacks on foreigners visiting the historical tourist sites in Egypt sharply affected income for the impoverished Egyptian state. It meant that unemployment remained high, and the unemployed were targeted by the fundamentalist Islam leadership as recruits against the secular government. The government pressed its attack against the insurgent religious factions, often crushing civil rights in the process. By the year 2064, the two sides were at a stalemate.

It would take a lot of innocent blood to snap that stalemate.

The University of Cairo had established a model campus on the outskirts of the sprawling city. The campus made use of much of the communications highway technology that was rapidly growing in places around the world. A major feature of the campus was that it was linked to the main campus in Cairo by a series of television cameras throughout the campus and inside the classrooms.

The electronic hookup and the awesome displays of computer wizardry that were showcased by students at the campus enraged local fundamentalist mullahs. These local religious leaders decried the electronics and computer technology as playthings of Satan and demanded that God-fearing Muslims eradicate the poison in their midst. The chief mullah of the suburban area where the school was located led a mob of more than a thousand fanatic followers onto the campus, overpowering the few guards. The shrieking mob, brandishing swords and rifles, cut down and mutilated scores of students—not realizing that their brutal handiwork was being taped and televised across the city and around the world (in a grisly public relations coup, the Egyptian government allowed CNN to tap into the feeds from the campus where the attack was broadcast live around the world). The horrifying attacks against the unarmed students, including many young women who were dismembered on camera, sickened the whole of Egypt and the rest of the world. The actions of the fundamentalists were so brutal and so undeniable that even pro-fundamentalist leaders elsewhere in the nation were forced to condemn the actions. Vengeful countermobs of friends and families of the students were assisted by local authorities in locating the ringleaders of the assault on the university branch.

The attack cut the moral heart out of the fundamentalist campaign. Gut-wrenching photographs of the atrocities were shown by counterdemonstrators at every fundamentalist rally, forcing the fundamentalists into a defensive stance. You can't rally your forces when you have to apologize for your actions first. Within three years, the fundamentalists had been beaten into submission. Their leaders were either in jail or in graves, and their rallies were greeted by more anti-fundamentalists than supporters. Their funding disappeared, and shortly after that so did the entire movement in Egypt.

The end of the fundamentalists' drive in Egypt also put the final nails in the coffin of similar fundamentalist movements throughout the Muslim world. Even in Iran where clerics had held sway for nearly one hundred years a secular government was elected despite religious activists' contentions that a return to rule by the people rather than by the mullahs would be tantamount to electing the devil.

The advent of the universally applied communications highway in the United States and abroad had other effects on organized religion. Television evangelists eagerly embraced the highway's potential because they saw a much larger audience. What they also found was that there was a geometric progression in the number of competing evangelists who now had access to the vast audience. Everyone's share diminished, as did their proceeds. By 2030, one evangelist after another was bowing out of the limelight. Several major television preachers held sway, but only for a few months before the void was filled by others. What seemed to elude all the preachers was that the number of people tuning in was getting smaller and smaller as their audience began exploring the never-ending universe of the communications highway that had opened before them. The numbers of evangelists plying the airwaves rose and fell like deregulated airlines in the 1980s. But the influence the TV preachers once held in the late twentieth century was never achieved in the twenty-first century—especially after the 2040s.

The major religious conflicts in the twenty-first century were the same conflicts that plagued mankind in the twentieth century: Islam vs. Christianity; Islam vs. Judaism; Judaism vs. Christianity; Catholicism vs. Protestantism. The main reason for conflict was the fact that there was almost daily interplay among the various religions. In more homogeneous religious areas—China and Japan, for instance—inter-religious strife was limited. Religious battles between Muslims and Hindus on the Indian subcontinent went unabated, making the twenty-first century no different than preceding millennia.

The most interesting attempt in the twenty-first century to limit the role of religion in affecting world events was tried by some of the colonists on Mars who in 2077 declared Ares City to be a Religion-Free Zone—forbidding the practice of religion, the uttering of religious curses, or the defining of anyone's character by associating a religious creed. The experiment lasted a month before the citizens of Ares City—the second largest community on Mars—realized how ridiculous it was to try to restrict religion. The community went overboard in correcting itself, and attempted to be the first completely Religious Strife-Free Zone. An octagonal-shaped chapel was constructed, giving every practicing religious rite at the time a place to hold religious services. It became a model of how people could actually live together despite having different beliefs.

The Guide gave up his reverie and turned away from the doors of the church—he pointed out the statuette in the image of Kateri Tekakwitha in the door.

"The Ares City chapel," he said, "became a shrine to brotherhood. It was a herald to what many in 2090 thought would be a world and a universe of brotherly love and harmony. It was, of course, just another pipe dream."

17

A NEW HAWAII

THE GRUBBY MAN WALKED WITH GLAZED EYES ALONG the sidewalk in Greenwich Village. He wore a sandwich board that proclaimed numerous passages from the Bible—or at least stated that these were biblical passages. In large letters the board read: PREPARE FOR THE END OF THE WORLD.

The sight of such a proclamation being carried by similar-looking men or women is not uncommon in New York City or even Greenwich Village for that matter. But as the September drizzle matted the few strands of his unkempt hair, I could feel a trembling in my legs. A shudder passed through my body and suddenly I felt terribly cold, as if an Arctic gale had forced the dampness of the day through my skin and deep into my bones.

I stared into the prophet's eyes and watched in fascination as the periphery of my vision began to lose color, then turn brown and then black. Rapidly and geometrically the darkness began to spiral to the center of my field of vision. I was transfixed by those slate-blue eyes that failed to notice my existence. As I began to wobble, I felt a strong arm grab my right elbow and steady me. I reached out and found a street lamppost and I hugged it for support.

As I caught my breath, I saw a gigantic wave appear out of the ocean and head straight towards me. The wave moved with brutish force. I could see debris— wood, vehicles, trees—in the wave. I covered my face instinctively and held my breath as the water crashed over me. I watched in horror as the wave grabbed the soothsayer of doom and carried him away. And then I watched in disbelief as the wave vanished, leaving the streets of Greenwich Village as grimy as ever.

It doesn't take a rocket scientist to figure out that what I had just experienced was a psychic dream, a hint of the future, another warning about a tragedy that would take place. But when? I asked myself.

I remembered the strong arm that held me up as I was about to pass out. I slowly turned around, and standing a couple of feet away, still dressed in his native garb, was the Guide. He glistened as the rain covered his body and soaked his clothes. My first thought, of course, was Aren't you cold?

He reached out for my hand on the crowded street. I extended my arm to him and felt his powerful grasp. I glanced around to see how many pedestrians noticed this bizarre woman reaching out for someone who wasn't there. One man arched his eyebrows and then looked away as he spotted his subway entrance and disappeared below the city streets without turning back; a child craned her head to watch me grasp at the air and kept staring until her mother pulled her forcefully across the street during a break in the traffic. Otherwise, I was ignored.

Because the Guide was present I concluded that my vision was connected with the warnings I'd received from Auriesville, and I thought about the writings. Yes, I thought to myself, I wrote about a flood, a disaster. As I thought about it, I could feel the humid warmth of a summer day, I could feel the burning sun that reminded

me of my trips to Florida, I could see the blue-green
waters of a tropical lagoon.

"Palmyra." I heard a voice and realized that it was
the Guide.

Now I was confused. For Palmyra is a well-known
land among psychics and those who deal with the ancient
world of gods and long-dead religions. I had been curious
about historical Palmyra for many years. I knew that it
was an ancient city state, possibly as much as four thousand years old. It was the center of a sun god-based
religion for centuries, before it was overrun by Arabs,
Romans, Greeks. Among its gods was the famous Baal,
lord of eternity, and one of the frequent answers to clues
in the Sunday *New York Times* crossword puzzle.

But I couldn't understand the context that Palmyra
had with the psychic visions. "If I haven't gone crazy," I said to myself, "these are supposed to be visions
of the future, not of the past." We had been walking back to my apartment. I still felt light-headed, so
I flopped on the sofa as soon as I had finished the
New York City ritual of unlocking the door and then
locking it behind me with a series of deadbolts and
latches.

The Guide ambled to my bookcase and found an atlas.
He returned to the sofa and sat down beside me, flipping
the pages of the book of maps until he came to the massive picture of the Pacific Ocean. "Hawaii," he pointed
out as if he knew that geography wasn't a strong point
of my academic training. He traced his finger southeast
of Hawaii to what looked like a dot in the middle of the
ocean. It was a dot in the middle of the ocean, and it
was called Palmyra.

The light went on in my brain. I eyed the Guide
cautiously because he often tested me. "The wave, the
destruction I felt on the street. That's going to happen
on Palmyra, this island in the Pacific. It has to do with
a disaster on this island, and doesn't have anything to
do with religion or Palmyra in the Middle East."

He held up his hand. "Yes, it has to do with the island, but it also has everything to do with religion," he said. He gripped my arms tightly and a flow of thoughts poured from him to me. Almost instantly, a strange scenario blossomed in my mind as I grasped the truth about the disaster at Palmyra.

In 2043, a group of the richest entertainers and sports figures—including the former home run king of baseball and the sexiest movie star since Marilyn Monroe—announced that they were devotees of Baal and their incredible success was primarily based on their adherence to the hedonistic-capitalistic religion based on the ancient rituals of the pre-Christian Palmyrans who also worshiped Baal.

The Baalists were mocked and scorned by their contemporaries and colleagues, but since they were among the best, brightest, and wealthiest individuals in the world, they didn't really care that organized religion and even the man-on-the-street considered them at best as kooks and at worst as devils on earth. Their interest in the religion of Baal made them keenly aware of the ruins of Palmyra in Iraq as well as the island of Palmyra in the Pacific, which while claimed by the United States government and used for decades as a semisecret naval base, had been abandoned in 2019 when the US determined that its deep-sea sensors and its reconnaissance satellites made a listening station in the middle of the Pacific redundant.

The Baalists inquired about the possibility of buying the island and offered a cash-strapped United States government $4 billion for a ninety-nine-year lease on the property. Since the island was uninhabited, and was frequented only by a few lost seamen or an occasional tourist, the government accepted the offer of the Baalists in 2045, as long as the group agreed to maintain the government's emergency rescue beacons and to allow for government inspections of the property as the government deemed necessary.

The Baalists began moving to Palmyra the following year, and by 2054, more than 1,200 men, women, and children were living there. The Baalists claimed that they were elite—by nature of the fact that nobody there was worth less than $100 million—and that they could foresee the future. They claimed that the world was about to end and that only the sun god Baal could save the world. Generally, they were ignored, although the slugger's baseball memorabilia sold for small fortunes and the sex goddess's films were always packed and rentals of her videos were always at the top of the lists.

"Actually," the Guide said, "the Baalists probably knew what they were doing. But like many false prophets, they misread the signals they were receiving or they ignored the advice of their guides or they thought they could change the world and change the forces of nature just through their own will. And that's why they died."

In 2051, the long-dormant volcano of Haleakala on the island of Maui erupted. Scientists had been studying Haleakala for centuries and seismic devices foretold of the pending eruption a decade earlier when it became apparent that the volcano had determined that it had been sleeping long enough. The eruption, while spectacular, and filed on videotape from one hundred different angles by thousands of cameras, was not particularly devastating. Residents had been given days of warning and even the most stubborn nay-sayers had decided to be cautious rather than be dead. The only victims were a few campers who had managed to sneak past federal guards, a few of the guards themselves, and a couple of unlucky scientists who were setting up equipment when the eruption occurred literally under their feet.

The eruption of Haleakala was followed by considerable volcanic activity on the big island of Hawaii where impressive volcanic eruptions had been occurring since the 1970s. But scientists on the big island of Hawaii were now concerned about seismic rumblings they were reading south of Hawaii in the area of the Pensacola Seamount, about two hundred miles due south of Hawaii.

Ominously, early in 2054, there was a significant lull in volcanic activity in the Hawaiian islands, and even on other areas of the Pacific "Ring of Fire." Scientists warned of the strong potential of a particularly mighty eruption and many predicted the blast could be in the Pensacola Seamount. Scientists noted that the Hawaiian island group geologically was building toward the south. The Necker Islands, north and east of Kauai, were the remains of ancient, dead volcanoes. The string of Hawaiian islands—Kauai, Oahu, Molokai, Maui, Lanai, and Hawaii—were relatively new land masses, with Hawaii the youngest of the islands, and still growing. The general opinion was that the next Hawaiian island would appear to the south and east of the big island of Hawaii. The location of the Pensacola Seamount was right in the path of where a new island would form if there was going to be another Hawaiian island.

A few months after the lull was first observed, a gigantic volcanic eruption occurred 203 miles south-southeast of the big island of Hawaii in the center of the Pensacola Seamount. Even though the top of the seamount was still hundreds of feet below the surface of the Pacific, the enormous strength of the eruption spewed volcanic gases and rocks thousands of feet into the atmosphere, vaporizing water as the molten rock from the center of the earth surged to the surface at supersonic speeds. The immense explosion displaced billions of gallons of water, creating a tsunami or tidal wave more than one hundred feet high. The wave diminished in size rapidly, but waves more than fifty feet high crushed the southern coast of Hawaii. Although protected somewhat by the direction of the waves, the city of Hilo was devastated and loss of life was in the hundreds when mountainous waves up to twenty feet high plowed through the city; Oahu and the other islands were similarly hammered—the waves destroyed the Battleship Arizona monument in Pearl Harbor and wiped the Honolulu airport into oblivion less than twenty minutes after the eruption took place, three hundred miles away.

The tsunami continued across the Pacific in all directions. Tidal waves crushed piers and marinas as far away as northern California; the waves caused oil spills in Alaska when it battered offshore oil facilities south of Anchorage; hundreds of people died in the deltas of Southeast Asia and walls of water as high as eight feet slammed into boat communities, turning junks into trash. But it was the Pacific Ocean atolls and islands where death charged ashore with churning waves as high as two-story buildings that flattened anything built along the shore.

The tsunami warnings that were sent out around the world kept loss of life at a minimum, although the low-lying atolls were battered beyond recognition. The warnings were received at Palmyra atoll, some 950 miles southwest of the eruption. Unencumbered by any land masses and slowed only by gravity, the tsunami that was one hundred feet high when the volcano erupted in the Pensacola Seamount was now forty-five feet high when it approached Palmyra, only an hour after the eruption.

The Baalists had yachts and ships and even some private aircraft that could have been utilized to try and save some of the hundreds of people on the island, but when the seamount erupted the entire community was in the middle of their three-hour daily ritual of prayer and tribute to the sungod. There was no one monitoring the emergency signals so the first time anyone realized there was a problem was when they looked up from their open-air prayer meeting on one of the atoll's islets and saw the water from the lagoon seemingly race out to sea.

A few moments after this phenomenon was recognized by the Baal faithful, they saw the massive tidal

wave blotting out their view of the morning sun. The
wave passed over the island as if it did not exist. All
the luxury boats and communal houses and temples to
Baal were scoured from the atoll and crushed into splin-
ters. The people of the community never had a chance.
There were no survivors; few of their bodies were ever
found, including the leaders of the Baalist revival, leading to years-long speculation and sightings—similar to
the so-called Elvis sightings of the 1980s.

The eruption at the seamount continued for months,
and eventually the flows of lava broke the surface—a
new island was created. The island was immediately
claimed by the United States and became part of the
state of Hawaii. The island continues to grow through
the years as the volcano continues to send magma from
the center of the earth to the surface. The island grows
into a curious birdlike shape, and the Hawaiians name
the island Nene, after the state's official bird.

It is years before anyone can settle on the island,
although scientists and volcanists set up remote machinery that can put the researchers—by using virtual-reality
software and robots with the latest in fireproof metals—
literally in the mouth of the volcano. The pictures from
the robots are so interesting and breathtaking that they
are broadcast on a dedicated cable channel. The Volcano Channel is so mesmerizing that parents complain
that their children are staying up all night to watch the
natural fireworks.

The first permanent settlement on the volcanic island
of Nene is established in 2098. The small community
of scientists—geologists and volcanists, mainly—set up
houses on the northern tip of the island, far from the
sulfuric fumeroles that smoke constantly on the southern end of the island that continues to add land mass
just about every day.

The death of the Baalists, which robbed the world of
many of its idols, begins a long period of antireligious
feeling in the world. The antireligionists point to the

worshipers of Baal as examples of how religion has warped the minds of some of the world's greatest geniuses and therefore has stolen precious abilities from the rest of the populace. On every continent, the antireligionists rail against any form of organized piety.

"Religion," the Guide said, "has always been a good reason for hating your neighbor. In the 2060s, with religion taking a worldwide backseat in the affairs of man, there had to be something else available to create mayhem. And naturally mankind found issues of race, ethnicity, sex, language, or something else to fight over."

I pondered his statements. "So by the end of the twenty-first century, there will be no religions? No more churches, no synagogues, no temples?" I suggested.

"No," he said. "The antireligionists will hold sway for a while but in 2074, antireligionism will be exposed as a religion itself and more traditional religions which were down but not out will reassert themselves among the population.

"Mankind will never escape its need to worship something."

18

MISSION TO THE STARS

IN 2090, THE FIRST REPORTS OF THE REMARKABLE EIGHT-
een-year-old IBM-Exxon Journey to the Stars Expedition will be received on Earth. The reports will tell of
amazing life on one planet surrounding the star, Alpha
Centauri, the nearest neighbor to our solar system.

The crew of the expedition, funded by giant corporations rather than by tax-strapped world governments,
headed to outer space from Spacebase Borneo in 2068.
On board were a crew of twenty—ten men and ten wom-
en who were matched for compatibility, intellect and
sexuality. The crew included space pilots, navigators,
doctors, engineers, and scientists.

The spaceship Explorer—no one ever said that businesses were original in naming products—was constructed in Earth orbit by the crews of the four space stations
circling earth. The fusion-powered engine system of the
Explorer was designed to continually accelerate the giant
ship. The total area of the ship would cover an acre
of land on Earth. Without the friction of a planetary
atmosphere, the ship is propelled faster and faster, reaching astounding speeds—but still nowhere near the light
speed envisioned in fictional "Star Trek" warp drives.

Because the trip through space is going to take years, there is extra space for the expected birth of children and the storage of remains of those who die either naturally or through accident.

Some experts predict that if the trip takes the estimated thirty-six years to complete its round trip to the nearest star, the crew of twenty will more than double by its return in 2104. Some people who were single when the crew left Earth will return as grandparents. Fears that pregnancy in space could be harmful to both mother and child had been proven wrong decades earlier during exploration to Jupiter and in couples who lived for long periods of time on the space stations.

It took the ship an entire year just to push beyond the gravitational pull of the solar system; years to negotiate the black space on the way to Sol's nearest neighbor, Alpha Centauri, 4.3 light years away. Telescopic improvements in the Hubble Telescope that were completed in the 1990s allowed scientists to locate planets on nearby star systems. The planets of Alpha Centauri seemed capable of supporting life.

But it still took half a century before politicians and the world's populace found the time and resources to send a research vessel out of our own solar system. The chaos of the asteroid divergence program of the 2040s delayed the Alpha Centauri project for twenty years but had the silver lining of developing technologies that made the Explorer mission possible.

Even after proving the worth of deep-space operations in our own solar system, there was terrific opposition to the probe to Alpha Centauri. The colonists on the Moon, although in place for twenty years, were clamoring for more funds to develop their perilous outposts. The Mars bases had similar demands, and the pioneering settlements on the moons of Jupiter thought it was ridiculous to explore outside the solar system when so much was left to be done in this system.

Others wondered why we would even think of exploring Alpha Centauri. Their arguments were simple: If there was any important intelligent life on Alpha Centauri's planets, then that life was either so far behind ours technologically that we would not gain anything from it, and Alpha Centauri would gain a giant boost in development from us without having to go through the struggles of learning to use technology. The argument continued that since there was no evidence of electronic development being transmitted from the Alpha Centauri system the chances of there being any developed life was slim indeed.

But big business came up with the money to fund the expedition after negotiating rights to whatever discoveries were made as long as those discoveries did not affect the development of intelligent species. The launch in 2068 was followed by weekly television reports. As the months slid by and the Explorer drifted farther and farther away, live television signals became less and less effective. It's tough to communicate with someone when you have to wait an hour for that person to hear your comment and then an hour to get a response.

After a year, reports were received as microburst information through computer systems. The reports interested scientists but were buried in newspapers and on news reports on television and computer news links. The scientists were gathering terrific data about the edges of the solar system and were already plotting new stars to visit on the next mission. Yet the mission was still light years away from the first objective, and a decade away from reporting on its findings.

Reports from the Explorer, which were being sent by the ship's crew on a daily basis, were now taking a year or two to reach earth. The births of the first children born on the journey made headlines, but as the 2080s rolled around, most people stopped worrying about or reading about the mission. Other events, such as baseball expansion, were of greater interest.

The Explorer actually reached the Alpha Centauri system in 2086, but no one on earth knew about it for four years, so 2090 is recorded as the date on which humans reached another solar system. Purists tried for years to get the world to agree that 2086 was really the proper date, but no one listened to that. People just remembered where they were and on what date when we found out that we were not alone in the universe.

On what would have been considered mid-summer of 2086 on Earth, the Explorer's unmanned mini-probe entered the atmosphere of the fourth planet of Alpha Centauri. It was the first planet discovered by the crew that showed any likelihood of having an atmosphere that could support some form of life. After a week of circling the planet from space orbit, the Explorer found no evidence of civilization, technology, or electronic development. There were water and land divisions and there was obvious volcanic activity across the face of the planet, which was roughly 20 percent larger than earth.

The mini-probe determined that the atmosphere on the planet was breathable, but had a higher concentration of oxygen than was found on earth. The planet had typical Earth-like weather formations—the probe picking up rain clouds, thunderstorms, cold fronts, and warm fronts. There were polar ice caps, although the intensity wasn't as strong as those on earth. There were jungles teeming with plants, and rivers and oceans. But there were no signs of civilization or intelligent life.

After another two weeks of preparations and study of the planet surface, five crew members took a probe to the surface of the planet. The crew spent much of the time locating a landing site to name the continents and oceans as is the prerogative of explorers. The landing was uneventful as the crew picked out a plateau in a desertlike area that was also within a hundred miles of a river basin.

It became apparent almost immediately upon landing and walking on the surface of the planet that there were life forms that existed all about them. Strange tracks crisscrossed the soil. The crew's protective spacesuits saved the explorers from attacks of a variety of flying and boring insectlike creatures. Many of them were venomous. They were frozen and embedded in paraffin to be shipped back to earth for study. The appearance of the bugs that obviously lived on the blood of other creatures sent the crew back to their probe in search of weapons. "What does a mosquito with a nine-inch wingspan feed on?" the crew chief on the ground asked rhetorically. The answer, of course, was something really big.

It took a couple of days of exploration before the crew discovered what was so big—dinosaurs. Or actually creatures the size of dinosaurs. Fortunately, the crew spotted the creatures from a distance of half a mile away. These were monsters that men on earth could not have dreamed. Some of them stood one hundred feet into the air and they moved with grace and speed. They could not have had any enemies, yet they approached the space crew—now hurrying back to the safety of their ship— with extreme caution.

From their vantage point in their landing craft, the crew photorecorded some of the strangest and most terrifying creatures—creatures that only nightmares could conjure. There was a forty-foot-tall beast with a square head and a huge maw. It wasn't a mouth as we know it, just an open space ringed by razorlike teeth. A crewman called it "Bladeface."

The crew watched in amazement as the creature spotted a mammalian form scurry across the arid plain. Bladeface fell to all fours and accelerated after the dog-sized furry critter—quickly called Ratdog. Bladeface lashed at Ratdog with a talon at the end of one limb covered with reptilian scales. A bloodlike substance of a purple rather than red color spurted from Ratdog as it collapsed to the ground. Bladeface kicked the downed animal, impaling the Ratdog on the pointed nail of its toe. In one motion, Bladeface flipped the dead prey into the air and it landed in Bladeface's maw. There was a splash of blood, a sucking noise, and the Ratdog was gone. When Bladeface turned to look at the landing craft, engines were fired immediately and the crew took off.

Flying at ten thousand feet, they located what seemed to be a safe landing place. They were unaware that this area, too, teemed with wildlife of super size. As the first crewman stepped out of the probe, three giant birds swooped down towards him at a speed in excess of one hundred miles per hour. The birds had wingspans that exceeded thirty feet but had no discernible head. The creature's eyes were placed strategically around a sharply curved beak from which protruded lancelike armor. The sudden attack caused a delay in the naming ceremony, but when the crew was able to gather its wits they called the creature a Maxieagle.

The crewman's partner saw the attacking birds first and didn't hesitate to fire her laser, burning the wing off the lead Maxieagle, which twisted through the air and then plowed into the ground. The other two birds continued their plunge at the crew. Another laser blast caught a second Maxieagle lead bird in the chest. It released a high-pitched, ear-splitting scream that forced the crewmen to wince in pain as their ears went numb. The injured Maxieagle, however, continued its plummet towards the crew. A giant talon of the dying bird slashed through the suit of the crew leader, causing severe arm and shoulder lacerations.

The third Maxieagle veered away, circling a thousand feet above the crew. Laser shots that hit the bird's wingtips and caused another mind-shattering howl got the message across, and the creature flapped into the distance.

The injured crewman was pulled back into the craft and the probe immediately returned to the Explorer. The injured crewman recovered.

The next day a well-armed expedition returned to the site of the attack with the idea of recovering the remains of the dead birds so that it could be studied on Earth. However, when they returned to the site they found only feathers and pieces of bone. The birds, which they estimated had a wingspan of thirty feet and must have weighed a couple of hundred pounds each, were missing.

Searching the area for signs of vulture or jackal carrion eaters, the crew was stunned to find what seemed to be crude cutting tools. They now assumed that there was some form of intelligent life on the planet, and began trying to locate that form. As other well-armed crews spread out across the planet recording signs of life, ores, and other resources, one group continued to hunt for the life forms that seemed to be tool makers.

The crew spotted another Ratdog and captured it, and then sacrificed it and left it near where the birds had fallen. Remote cameras equipped with fuzzy intelligence-programmed computers were secreted about to record the life forms that the crew hoped would be attracted to the kill. The cameras were self-propelled and were programmed to follow the creatures and report back to the probe. Within a few minutes after the humans left, forms appeared to rise out of the sandy desert floor. When later studied, the explorers realized that the bipeds had been watching for hours, cleverly camouflaged. Apparently, the reptilian and mammalian and avion creatures that abounded on the planet were—similar to Earth animals—only equipped to see moving objects.

The crew dubbed the bipeds Toolmakers. The bipeds approached the bait and butchered the creature swiftly. The Toolmakers had two eyes, two hands, and two feet, and walked on their feet. They seemed remarkably humanoid, but had immensely large shoulders and thighs. They were unclothed. Sexual organs also seemed humanlike. Both sexes were engaged in the hunt.

The cameras dutifully followed the group of Toolmakers toward a line of hills. The Toolmakers spotted the tailing cameras and attempted to capture the devices, but, of course, to no avail. They were successful in hitting the cameras with stones launched by hand or from slings, but the missiles did no damage. The cameras were programmed to back off if assaulted so they just used greater lens length to keep the Toolmakers in sight.

The cameras followed the Toolmakers to their home, a cave system in the hillside. The cameras were unable to follow into the cave because of a lack of lighting and because they were programmed not to be put in a position where capture was possible. From the position outside the caves, however, the cameras were able to register heat on their sensors that indicated that the Toolmakers knew how to use fire. The cameras positioned themselves outside the caves and recorded one apparent attack by wildlife that was beaten back by the Toolmakers using various forms of weaponry—spears, arrows, and stones. The opening to their cave would have permitted only small game to enter. The larger carnivorous beasts were kept at bay.

A scientific historian on board the Explorer was puzzled by the appearance of reptilian, mammalian, and humanoid life apparently living in the same time frame. He postulated that the planet didn't suffer the massive species killoffs that occurred on earth. No giant asteroid smashed into this planet causing a destruction of the food supply for the giant dinosaur-type creatures. Evolution continued at an Earth-like pace, but major species didn't die off. He theorized that the presence of the giant reptiles prevented the humanoid population from building cities or even tending farms or developing weapons that could defeat the larger creatures.

The location of apparently intelligent life forms created a serious problem for the Explorer. The crew realized that its presence on the planet could upset

the intellectual balance and could change the development of the planet. They also found that the
planet was extremely rich with the types of resources
desired on earth. There was serious debate about leaving a small outpost on the planet but that was
rejected. The crew of twenty had now swollen to
a crew of forty-five—twenty-seven members being
born in space, less two men who died in an accident
onboard.

The return to Earth was going to take another eighteen
years and a return trip to the planet would be eighteen
years later than that. So if an outpost were put in place
on the planet, it would be thirty-six years before it could
be resupplied. Too many bad things could happen in that
time frame to make it feasible to leave the crew there.
So the Explorer returned home with its entire crew.

The initial reports that reached Earth in December
of 2090 electrified the world. Immediately additional
ships were built to return to the planet, despite world
government demands that humans wait until after the
Explorers return, expected in 2104, so that the captured creatures could be examined and antidotes to
local diseases and venoms developed. Despite World
Space patrols, many private ships began the hazardous
journey to Alpha Centauri, hopeful of setting up claims
on what seemed to be a new, exciting planet.

The Guide looked at me as I studied the map of the
stars, trying to locate Alpha Centauri. "You know what
is going to happen on that planet, don't you?" he asked.
I looked at him puzzled. I had no answers and I saw
no reports. "No," I said. "I see nothing about that."

He hummpphhed. "What you should do is think of your
own history. Remember what happened when Columbus
came to America and others followed? What you should
do is go ask the Caribs what happened to them when the
Europeans came to America."

"The Caribs?" I asked. "Who are they? I've never
heard of them."

"The Caribs," the Guide sighed, "were the natives who populated the islands of the Caribbean."

"Oh," I said. I was going to ask where I can find a member of the Carib tribe to discuss that with, but he again read my thoughts.

"Don't bother," he said. "They are extinct."

19

BASEBALL

I AWAKENED—OR MORE LIKELY I THOUGHT I HAD awakened—to see my guide sitting on the edge of my bed. He was watching me, a curious glint in his eye, a slight smirk on his face. I don't know why but I immediately thought about my friend's cat, a fat-bellied Siamese that assumed that humans were put on earth to be slaves of the feline race.

The Guide stepped forward, his hands uncharacteristically behind his back. Then suddenly he pulled his left arm from behind him and in a flash raised it over his head and then down on my head as I started to sit up. There was something in his hand and then I felt something on my head—cloth. I reached up and touched the bill of the cap. I looked into the mirror on the bed: It was a baseball cap with a familiar "N" and "Y" intertwined. The Yankees, I thought.

He said, "We're going to the World Series." I looked at him askance. We've seen wars, famine, earthquakes, death, destruction, marvels of science—and now baseball. Why was this guide interested in baseball, anyway. He was dead two hundred years before the first pitch was allegedly thrown in Cooperstown in 1839.

As always, he knew my thoughts, and responded to them: "Baseball is the perfect sport. Like many I was first unconvinced when I first viewed the game. But I've come to find it to be a wonderful analogy of life. Success is determined by individual triumph against great odds—but only with a cooperative effort of all. It remains the most difficult of all sports—trying to hit a round sphere hurtling towards you in a split second with a round bat. Simple contact is failure; solid contact is usually failure; only a perfect stroke results in triumph—unless you have unusual luck. It is a humbling game that makes for sincere modesty among even the best of the players. The drama of the game—the part many people find the most boring—is heightened only by playing the game or understanding every nuance."

"This is all wonderful, but what does it have to do with the future, with the message to the world, with our warning?" I asked.

"Everything," he said. "No matter what has happened or what will happen, one thing will remain constant. The game. It will always be here and it will always triumph and it will always be the same. But where it's played will be different.

"We're going to watch the World Series in the year 2097. I don't know how it is going to end. I never ruin the enjoyment of the game by knowing the result. But I can tell you that it's been decades since the Yankees have made it to the championship game of the World Series—which really is a World Series by the end of the twenty-first century.

"The Yankees are playing the latest sports dynasty, the Holy Land Peacemakers, which rotates its games in stadiums in Jerusalem, Jericho, Beirut, and Cairo."

Despite the turmoil that the world has been through in the twenty-first century, the upheavals in governments and in the Earth itself, America's favorite pastime has not only survived, it has grown and expanded.

In 2097 there are eighty-four teams in major league

baseball, and the game is played on every continent, although professional baseball hasn't taken a toehold in Antarctica as yet. In addition to the major league levels there are literally thousands of minor leagues around the world.

The teams are divided into fourteen six-team leagues, in four divisions. The America East Division has three leagues: Northeast, Middle Atlantic, and South.

The Northeast is made up of the following teams: the Boston Red Sox, the Montreal Expos, the New York Yankees, the Toronto Blue Jays, the Pittsburgh Pirates, and the Buffalo Bisons.

The Middle Atlantic teams are the New York Mets, the Philadelphia Phillies, the Washington Reps, the Baltimore Orioles, the Charlotte Smokies, and the Atlanta Olympians. The Olympians were, of course, the Atlanta Braves, but the success of the 1996 Olympic Games in Atlanta and the increased pressure from Native American groups that despised the depiction of the Braves resulted in the name change. Unfortunately the change of name also corresponded to a change in fortunes for the baseball team that failed to live up to its new nickname. In one hundred years after the name change, the Olympians won their division only six times, and advanced as fast as the quarterfinals of the World Series tournament only twice.

The South teams are the St. Petersburg Pelicans, the Miami Marlins (when St. Pete entered the league the Marlins dropped the name Florida as a peace offering to the long-suffering St. Petersburg residents who built a ballpark in the 1980s and didn't get anyone to play in it for thirty years), the Havana Stogies, the San Juan Stars, the Santo Domingo Caribes (taking the name of an Indian tribe was considered patriotic in the Dominican Republic), and the New Orleans Deltamen (a name that the team retained even after the first women were playing the major leagues, and even after New Orleans had women playing for its squad).

Under rules established in the last reorganization and expansion in 2086, the America East Division and Eurasia, which also has three leagues, sent four representatives to the World Series tournament—the winners of the three divisions and the team with the next best record (to be decided by myriad tiebreaker considerations, none of which had been used in decades).

The America West Division is made up of four leagues: North Central, Plains-to-Gulf, Northwest, and Pacific.

The North Central teams are the Chicago White Sox, the Cincinnati Reds (the oldest professional team, which considered moving the franchise in 2015, but new management changed its mind when a mob aided by police kidnapped the team's managers and held them until they sold out to a new management group), the Cleveland Lakers (another team whose nickname ran afoul of political correctness), the Detroit Tigers, the Milwaukee Brewers, and the Minnesota Twins.

The Plains-to-Gulf teams are the Chicago Cubs (who didn't win their first World Series until the twenty-first century—my guide said it would be unfair even if it was cruel not to say when the Cubs would finally break the World Series drought), the St. Louis Cardinals, the Kansas City Royals, the Texas (Dallas–Fort Worth) Rangers, the Houston Astros, and the Winnipeg Plainsmen.

The Northwest teams are the Colorado (Denver) Rockies, who set a record unlikely to ever be broken by having 647 consecutive sellouts in their new stadium, the Vancouver, BC, Columbians (a nickname that has resulted in teams from Colombia boycotting major league baseball for more than fifty years), the Seattle Mariners, the San Francisco Giants, the Los Angeles Dodgers, and the Oakland A's.

The Pacific teams are the Honolulu Hawaiians (despite being scoffed at for coming up with one of the most obvious nicknames available, the Hawaiians caught on with the fans and the nickname was never replaced even though every time a new owner took over the team a contest was announced to find another name, unsuccessfully), the California (Anaheim) Angels, the San Diego Gulls (they dropped the historically correct Padres during the antireligion frenzy in the 2060s), the Mexico City Sols, the Managua Iguanas, and the Caracas Oilers.

The Eurasia division consists of the Europe West, Central, and Southeast leagues. The Europe West teams are the Berlin Panzers (the obvious objections to the name were beaten down by overwhelming fan support), the Budapest Magyars, the London Knights, the Rome Legions, the Milan Bankers (the team kept the nickname of the failed franchise in Geneva, Switzerland), the Casablanca Bogies (in the 2010s thousands of Americans, lured by the constant reruns of the movie *Casablanca*, made the Moroccan city a place to retire or flee family and debts, and virtually everyone opened a tavern which was called "Rick's" or "Cafe Americaine").

Even though the Bogies are the only franchise located in Africa (the Peacemakers only play a dozen games a year in Egypt), no one objects to their being in a league called Europe West. The Bogies are one of major league baseball's most successful franchises despite a relatively small population base. Every American-owned business in Casablanca closes during the games, assuring a massive crowd of rabid supporters.

The Central teams are the Warsaw Rebels (honoring the resistance fighters during Nazi occupation and the success of fighting communist oppression in the 1960s and 1970s—games between Warsaw and Berlin and Warsaw and Moscow at the Warsaw Stadium are featured by policemen on horseback who patrol foul territory), St. Petersburg Defenders (this is the Russian team, not a misplaced team from Florida), the Moscow Union (the only team in major league baseball without a plural nickname), the Bucharest Blues (a reference to the Danube River, which flows through the Romanian capital, a river which hasn't been the blue of song in a millennium due to pollution from a dozen countries), the Athens Sailors, and the Holy Land Peacemakers.

The Peacemakers were a natural occurrence following the expansion of 2031, which created sixteen new teams and made baseball an international game. So many Americans were living in Israel or the financial capitals of Palestine and Lebanon that the push for a team was intense. In keeping with the burgeoning international complexion of the Holy Land, the team came up with a remarkable marketing group—something borrowed from the defunct American Basketball Association in the 1960s that had a team that called several cities in the Carolinas "home." The Holy Land team plays alternate series in a new stadium outside Jerusalem in Israeli territory and also at the former Olympic stadium near Jericho. And reminiscent of the Brooklyn Dodgers who occasionally played some home games in New Jersey during the 1950s, the Holy Land team also scheduled as many as twelve games each year in Beirut's new ultradome, and a similar number of games in Cairo.

But the true success of Holy Land and its century-long reign as a baseball dynasty was the incredible financial backing the team received. Jewish businessmen around the world, and especially in the United States sent millions of dollars to be used by the team to get the best talent available. Arabs and Muslims who controlled billions in oil, real estate, and other interests matched the offers dollar for dollar, yen for yen.

In 2034, the Peacemakers spent $76 million more than the team's entire income from attendance and television broadcast rights thanks to generous baseball-loving fans who refused to let one ethnic group outspend the other. So financially irresponsible was the Peacemakers approach to hiring baseball talent that major league baseball was finally forced to impose a workable salary cap.

The Southeast teams are the Katmandu Snocaps (who psyched out pitchers for years by implying that the high

altitude of the nation of Nepal made baseballs fly farther and faster out of Katmandu's stadium while, in fact,
the city is located at an altitude lower than that of Denver—but it still doesn't explain why the Snocaps are pe-
rennial leaders in home runs), the Karachi Scimitars, the
Bangkok Explorers (the nickname is puzzling to many
who aren't sure why the name was chosen although
there are those who claim it involves the Thai capital's
late twentieth century reputation for having developed
new-to-the-world sexual encounters), the Saigon Trad-
ers, the Manila Greens (named by the multi-billionaire
owner of the team who happens to be an eccentric envi-
ronmentalist), and the Tokyo Dragons.

The Australasia Division includes the Islands, Japan,
China and Australia leagues. The Island league teams
are the Tokyo Lions, Osaka Kites, Taipei Eagles, Seoul
Choppers, Manila Bombers, and the Naha (Okinawa)
Lightning Bolts.

The Japan league teams are the Tokyo Wizards (now
the old song has to be rewritten because Tokyo is the only
city with three baseball teams), the Nagoya Hammers, the
Kocki Islanders, the Taipei Gunslingers (despite being
the only team in the Japan League not from Japan, the
Slingers used the jealousy and rivalry among the Japanese
teams to their advantage and win the league crown more
frequently than would be expected), the Nagasaki Crows,
and the Sapporo Gliders.

The China league teams are the Canton Roosters, the
Shanghai Horses, the Beijing Hams, the Nanking Cats—
all the Chinese teams entered the league separately and
took as a nickname the corresponding animal who was
honored that year by the Chinese calendar—the Seoul
Reindeers, and the Vladivostok Huskies.

The Australian league teams are the Sydney Roos,
the Adelaide Birds, the Perth Navigators, the Brisbane
Koalas, and the Canberra Stripers (named after the
multicolored striped socks worn by the players). Because
Australia is located in the Southern Hemisphere where it

is winter when the rest of the world is having spring or summer, each of the Australian league teams plays in a semidomed stadium, similar to Toronto's SkyDome. The stadium has a retractable roof that allows play under the sun or stars, weather permitting.

The World Series tournament involves sixteen teams. Each division seeds its team one through four and then by opponents are drawn from a hat—division versus division. In each division the number four seed plays its opposite number one team in a best of seven series.

When the eight teams remain, the teams are reseeded based on the season's won-loss record, with consideration taken as to whom was defeated in the round of sixteen. Again the lowest seed plays the first seed in a best of seven series.

The resulting four survivors then select their semi-final opponent by the luck of the draw. The best of seven winners of this series meet for the World Series final, which is played at a neutral site. Because the final series is usually not played until mid-December, warm weather sites with the required 100,000-seat stadium play host to the greatest sports event of the year. The games rotate among Stadio Beisbol outside Havana, Caracas Internacional in Venezuela, the Superdome in Melbourne, and La Grande Amphiteatre de Sportif in Casablanca.

20

CRIME PREDICTION

I AWOKE DEPRESSED.

The fate of the world seemed to rest upon my shoulders. No longer could I bear the burden of the visions that followed in my everyday footsteps. I became remorseful, afraid to go out, afraid to dream—afraid to be alive.

Then I saw a face of a child being carried into a hospital. The boy is just about four or five years old and tears and terror mark his face. His parents are with him. They're sophisticated, almost aristocratic in bearing, perhaps even serene. The specter of disease hovers over them, but I see a blue aura surrounding the child and a yellow light inside his body. He is sick, but whatever treatment he is getting is going to be successful.

The child will live, I said to myself, and then I began to wonder why I was being shown this image. Many children get sick and then get better. Why is this child special? I asked myself as the image faded. Is he going to be a world leader? Is this the scientist who will find an answer to the plagues of the world?

I could see in the corner of the image a clock. I quickly recognized that the clock was pointing towards midnight; I could see the ball dropping from the Times

Square tower. And the date at the bottom read "1998."
I meditated, and swirling pictures flashed past me as if
I was watching a movie at warp speed. It was a horror
movie.

Early in the first decade of the twenty-first century,
crime and the threat of violence create an era of dread
in America. The possibility of becoming an instant vic-
tim of crime is even money any time a person walks
outside in a large metropolitan city. City governments,
strapped for cash and tax dollars, cannot cope with the
avalanche of criminal activity. Companies hire bodyguards to escort customers and employees from buildings to taxicabs—and then hire snipers to protect the
bodyguards.

Even in suburban areas, no home is secure without
paid bodyguards to keep criminals from attacking residents as they emerge from vehicles—either their own
safety cars or a public transport that is armed to the
teeth. Despite the requirements of armored vehicles,
personal palmprint ignition devices, and a daunting
array of sophisticated prevention mechanisms, crooks,
car thieves, and carjackers still terrorize America.

Despite this, there is no concentrated effort to crack
down on the criminal activity, until the crime of the century occurs in 2005. Carjackers kill two bodyguards, and
kidnap, torture, rape, and murder the wife and two pre-
teen daughters of a popular US senator at their home in
suburban Denver. The three vicious criminals, each with
a long history of violent crime, then escape attempts to
capture them and go on a month-long spree of murder and robbery across Nebraska, South Dakota, and
Minnesota before they are finally captured without a
struggle outside of Rochester, Minnesota.

They are convicted and sentenced to die in three states
but as they are being transported under heavy guard to
prison in Colorado, their criminal friends attack the prison convoy with heavily armed helicopter gunships that
have been stolen from a military base. The ensuing

firefight results in the deaths of thirty-five law enforcement officers as well as the three convicted murderers whose bus explodes in flame during the battle. The helicopter is shot down by air force planes that are scrambled from a nearby base.

The uproar over the original crimes and the shootout near Greeley set the stage for drastic changes in America's fight against crime. The fears, worries, and screams of overreaction by civil libertarians are outshouted by crime-weary citizens. A series of legislative and constitutional changes are swept into law—the most important of the changes is an amendment to the Constitution that strips felons of their civil rights while serving sentences for crimes.

Immediately, huge prisons are built in desolate areas of the nation. With their access to civil rights eliminated, prisons no longer have to provide state-of-the-art comfort in prison cells. Air-conditioning, television, recreational facilities, and legal libraries are no longer required for prisons. Cells are made smaller, facilities are more spartan and therefore less expensive, and prisoners are required to perform work tasks while confined. Sentences are stiffer and paroles more difficult.

The impact on crime, however, is negligible. Even with changes in laws that make convictions easier by relaxing some rules of evidence, street crime continues to be an uncontrollable problem throughout America.

In 2010, a young child—the same one who needed experimental brain surgery in 1998—starts tinkering with a computer model. He is especially interested in law—his uncle is a policeman—and artificial intelligence. He is attracted to devices that began appearing in cities in the 1980s. These devices were cameras that were placed above traffic lights to capture vehicles that violated traffic laws. The devices were remarkable in their ability to capture details such as license plates, determine speed, and even observe features with enough clarity to identify the driver.

However, the devices were expensive, and except for a rare occurrence in which the camera caught a car striking a pedestrian, the information the cameras gave the law enforcement officers was limited in use. The cameras had to catch hundreds of violators to pay for themselves, but when people learned of the cameras' existence, the traffic signals were obeyed. But the cost of maintenance proved too expensive for the devices to be used extensively.

But this child, Arthur, starts theorizing. What about the use of four television cameras hooked into one light at an intersection so that the cameras can see in all directions? What if that camera can send its information through a digital signal that can be monitored at a central place? What if every intersection had such a camera?

Working quickly and getting help from anticrime forces, the young computer wizard feeds his computer definitions and descriptions and enactments of criminal activity—from purse snatching to a driveby shooting. The computer is developed along the lines of fuzzy logic, which allows the computer to "think" and discover what is meant by crime and to recognize it when it happens.

With the network of cameras in place and the computer logic at work, the computer is able to spot crime anywhere on the street, identify the participant, and determine which participant is the criminal. With exacting clarity, the television cameras can follow the criminal down the street and inform the observers at the next intersection to monitor the progress of the criminal.

Meanwhile, the central computer is storing the data—the crime and the flight of the criminal—and has broadcast an alert to police about the crime, the exact position and movements of the criminal, and has broadcast the criminal's picture to televisions or fax machines in police cars.

Street crime becomes ancient history overnight. With evidence of the crime on videotape, its authenticity ensured by myriad backup sensors, the prosecutors have no trouble convicting anyone spotted by the crimestopping television cameras.

There are cries everywhere that the cameras represent "Big Brother" at his worst. That everyone's freedoms are being destroyed by the devices. But the public ignores these protests due to the incredible early work done by judges and lawyers to make sure that the computers can only locate and follow violent crimes. If the computer makes a mistake—for example, thinking the public and loud affections of a couple represent a sexual attack—the entire tape of the proceeding is erased.

The system works. Not only are the criminals arrested and convicted, the reforms in the criminal justice system mean that when they are convicted the criminals go to jail. Even with relaxed rules on what constitutes a proper jail, there are so many people convicted and sentenced to long terms that space becomes cramped. In a major move, the US government turns St. Lawrence Island in the north Pacific into a giant prison. It becomes Alcatraz multiplied a thousand times. But it has the space for tens of thousands of criminals and is virtually escapeproof—it is dubbed America's Devil's Island "without the ambiance."

Within a couple of years, the city streets are safe— even at night. Decent, law-abiding citizens finally get to take back their streets. And business booms.

Arthur is honored everywhere and becomes a national hero. But by the time he finishes his college career in 2018 and gets his doctorate in computer science, he is virtually a forgotten figure. He goes on to be a successful businessman, but never reaches the popularity he had as a teenager.

Crime, however, disappears from the streets of America. The system that Arthur devised becomes standard in every city in the United States and in many metropolitan areas around the world.

Even in suburban and rural America the system is in

place, and only on long stretches of lonely highways are Arthur's sentinels not in place. But those areas are crime-free too. The roads are lonely because no one lives there—not even crooks.

21

CONCLUSION

THE CRACK OF THE BAT MOMENTARILY HUSHED THE huge crowd. Then, as if a giant puppeteer was controlling the vast assemblage, everyone rose as if they were part of a giant tidal wave. A harsh, near-barbaric crescendo erupted from one hundred thousand throats as the tightly wound baseball headed toward left-centerfield in a huge parabolic flight.

The fleet-footed centerfielder raced toward the dark green padded wall, gliding across the blue-green outfield carpet with ever-lengthening strides. His left foot touched the brown dirt of the warning track. His right foot planted in the middle of the track, he launched his body in a seemingly impossible stretch up, up, and up to the top of the fence. The white baseball and the brown glove appeared to intersect at the same spot just as the outfielder crashed against the fence, his back taking the entire brunt of the force. He slowly slumped to the earth, disappointment etched on his face so deeply it was apparent three hundred feet away.

The crowd exploded as the batter leapt for joy midway between first and second base. I wasn't emotionally involved—it's tough to know who to root for when the

206

teams are playing one hundred years in the future. I cheered the thrill of the moment and the excellence of the play and turned to see if the Guide was enjoying the game as well.

But sitting next to me was a three-hundred-pound, red-faced and gray-bearded man, screaming so loud it seemed the veins in his neck would explode. I blinked and I was staring into the dark. The glow of the familiar electric clock at the side of my bed let me know that I was home, in my bedroom. I was alone.

Confused and alarmed, I got up and walked around the room. Was that a dream? I thought. I really was at a baseball game, I reasoned with myself. I began to have self-doubts. Every time I had seen the Guide, I had been awake. I had never dreamt about him. Or had I always dreamt about him? I asked myself. I sat in the dark on the edge of the bed. I reached for the baseball cap the Guide had given me. But all I could find on my head was my hair, scraggly from sleep. Cautiously, I lay back down on the bed. I stared at the ceiling for several minutes. I could feel my heart beating wildly. I could almost hear my heart beating through my nightgown. Slowly I closed my eyes. Eventually I slept. I didn't dream.

I awoke to a drizzly Saturday morning. I cursed the weather. "It only rains in New York City on weekends," I muttered as I got up and went on my normal Saturday routines inside and outside the apartment. Occasionally the mystery of the previous night would invade my thoughts, but I put it aside. There are a number of chores that I do on Saturdays that I can't put off. "If it's really important," I rationalized, "the Guide will show up. He's got his own schedule."

Saturday slid into Sunday, and then the work week began afresh. It wasn't until Wednesday that I realized that I hadn't seen the Guide since the trip to the baseball game. Or was that just a dream? Every time I heard a noise in the apartment or saw the briefest flurry of movement outside, I relaxed and waited for his appearance. I scanned the faces of the people walking down the street, trying to see his hard features in an unlikely outfit.

I returned to my apartment Wednesday night and went over to the computer and started writing what I remembered of the dream—I was practically convinced now that it had been a dream—and the state of baseball in the twenty-first century. It came so easily to me that I dropped my belief of a dream and again put faith in the probability that it was the Guide who had taken me out to the old ball game. My fingers flew over the keyboard as the leagues and divisions were recalled. I had found over the weeks of working with him that after receiving the messages of the Guide I was able to transform them to words and thence to the computer disc with little effort. If something seemed unclear or my memory was vague, I could refer to my book of automatic writings that I had begun so feverishly after that extraordinary event at Auriesville. And if neither worked, I could self-activate a trance or employ a friend to assist me in pulling out all the information that was whirling in my subconscious.

Suddenly I felt a sick feeling in the pit of my stomach. I turned from my computer to the table next to the sofa where I always placed the book—that all-important book stuffed with pages that had torn free of the wire rings and the napkins on which I had scrawled impossible notes as I rode south on the New York State Thruway eight months before. The book wasn't there. I felt a bead of sweat roll down my back; my heart rate increased; my breathing became short. Don't panic, Shawn, I told myself, the book is here.

I got up from the computer, stopped and returned to the keyboard, and pressed the buttons to save what I had written. A fear crossed my mind. I removed the disc from the computer drive and pressed the tiny square against my chest. I carefully placed it in the disc drawer. I got back up and walked over to the table. The book obviously wasn't there. No papers were on the table, just a lamp. I felt foolish, but I lifted the lamp to see if the book had somehow found its way under its base. Of course, it wasn't there.

The last time I remembered seeing the book it was on the table. I could see myself come inside the apartment and remove the book from my purse and place it on the table. Maybe, I considered, I am thinking of a different time and place. I picked up my brown purse and searched it. The book wasn't there. I took the purse to the kitchen table and dumped it out, scurrying to catch rolling tubes of lipstick before they crashed to the tile floor.

I carefully separated the contents. (I would eventually discard about a pound and a half of junk and used-up cosmetics: Everything has a silver lining, I reminded myself.) There was no book there.

I went to my closet and opened up every purse I owned. Some of the purses were empty. I turned them inside-out to be sure they were empty. The others were taken to the table for another search and destroy mission. I found myself biting my lip and my eyes were beginning to water. Something deep inside of me told me that if I couldn't find the book something terrible was going to happen.

There was no book in any of the purses. I glared at my closet, willing it to tell me where the notebook was hidden. An answer appeared: My coat pocket. I yanked my favorite wool coat off its hanger and frisked it. No book. I turned the pockets inside out. No book. I tossed the coat on the couch and pulled another coat out of the closet. Its hanger clattered to the floor. No book. When I had gone through all the coats, jackets and robes, I flopped down on the floor amidst the jumble of clothes and dropped my head into my hands.

Get a hold of yourself, I told myself. I picked myself up and began returning the clothing to the closet. As I put the garments on the hangers, I went through the pockets one more time. Darkness was settling on Greenwich

Village, matching my despair. I called up my business partner who often has guided me through the forests of my own creation.

"I think I'm going crazy," I told her. I explained about the Guide, about the book, about everything I had been going through the last few hours. I must have talked for twenty minutes before she broke in.

"Let me get this straight, Shawn," she said. "You think you are going crazy because the ghost that has been tagging along with you for the past few months is no longer showing up? You know, most people would think that not having a ghost around is normal, not abnormal."

We both laughed. But I quickly became serious again. "But what about the book? You saw me writing the book? Please, tell me you saw me writing the book?"

"Sure. Of course I remember. For a week that's all you did. I don't even remember you getting anything to eat. By the way, did I tell you that you looked really good after that week? You must have lost ten pounds. Starvation does a lot for a person's figure."

We chuckled again, and I felt a lot better. At least someone knew that I had been engaged in writings—that wasn't a figment of my imagination. The Guide, of course, never appeared when anyone I knew was around, and I always had the good sense and good graces not to introduce him to strangers—who couldn't see him anyway.

"Well," I told my friend, "at least I know that I did write it. Now I just wish I could find it."

"Where did you last leave it?"

"Well, I thought I left it on the table. You know, I've showed you the book there a dozen times," I said.

"Yes, and all the times that you explained what those squiggles meant I nodded as if I understood what you were saying. You knew, Shawn, that I had no idea what you were talking about?"

"Yes," I admitted, "I knew that."

She laughed. "So, I suppose you looked under everything on the table."

"Of course," I said impatiently.

"And you looked under the table, too, I suppose?"

I froze. "Hold on," I said sheepishly.

I got down on my knees and crawled under the table. There was no book there either. I reached around the corners of the sofa next to the table, but the book wasn't there either. I reached under the sofa. Nothing. I walked over to the kitchen cabinets and opened one of the drawers and pulled out a flashlight.

I returned to the living room and lifted up the fabric skirt covering the sofa. I got down on my knees and then lay prone, my cheek plastered against the hardwood floor. I held the skirt with my left hand and with the right I slowly, deliberately cast the light's beam under the sofa. No book.

But something else was under the sofa. I dropped the skirt and with my left hand I reached for the object and pulled it out. It was a white and black, seven-inch-long bird feather. As I grasped the perfectly formed feather, meaning flowed to me.

Holding the feather in front of me, I walked back to the telephone. "No," I said, "the book wasn't there. But I think I know where it is. Thanks for helping." I hung up as my friend sputtered something like "don't leave me hanging like . . ."

I sat down on the sofa and twirled the feather in front of me. "So, you took the book. You took away any proof I might be able to show that something had indeed happened to me at Auriesville and afterwards. You are truly fiendish, my guide that I'll never see again."

As I sat immersed in my thoughts, I remembered the computer. If the Guide could take my book, what was going to stop him from wiping out the computer, too? With trepidation I called up the files on the computer that I had been writing immediately after something the

Guide said or something I had figured out on my own became clear.

Every night I had punched into the computer my thoughts or fragments of conversations with the Guide. I had taken to heart what he had said about not being certain when he would return or even if he would ever return. There was still plenty of information there that I thought I could decipher on my own if I ever needed to.

I sighed deeply. The directory of files showed that everything I had written was still there. I began recalling them one by one to make sure that the bytes were still in the order I had written them. They were. I felt overwhelming relief. Then I thought I recalled something in the directory. The hair on the back of my neck stood straight up. I went back into MS-DOS and asked for a directory of files again. There it was: A file I didn't put in the computer. I called it up—it was very short.

"Remember, you are the voice of the prophets. I am your Guide but I am directed by the prophets as well. You don't need any props or totems to tell your story. Just tell it and the people will either believe it and save themselves or they will ignore it and continue on the path to the Apocalypse that awaits the planet. There is plenty to cheer about in the twenty-first century and there is much heartbreak as well.

"Remember Jonah. Help the people help themselves. Make them change to prove you are wrong. God help them if they don't."

22

CHRONOLOGY

2000

Scientists announce new medications and new genetically engineered therapies that eliminate—in 95 percent of the cases—organ rejection, allowing for more and safer organ transplant operations. Finding donor organs remains a problem, however.

2001

The admission of Puerto Rico as the fifty-first state at the turn of the century begins a neo-nationalistic, imperialistic drive in the United States.

2003

Helicopters crash into fuel tanks adjacent to a huge shopping mall in Syracuse, NY. More than one thousand people doing last-minute Christmas shopping are killed.

2005

The crime of the century. Carjackers kill two bodyguards, and kidnap, torture, rape, and murder the wife and two pre-teen daughters of a popular US senator near their home in suburban Denver. The three vicious criminals, each with a long history of violent crime, then escape attempts to capture them and go on a month-long spree of murder and robbery across Nebraska, South Dakota, and Minnesota before they are finally captured—without a struggle outside of Rochester, Minnesota.

A dying heart researcher secretly inoculates his son with pig protein, knowing that his son will develop a similar disease—a disease that destroys the heart. The researcher will hope that the inoculation will mean that in thirty years his son could have a pig heart transplant and not have to worry about a shortage of human organs.

The former Soviet republic of Kazakhstan emerges as an economic force. The nation uses its mineral wealth and a democratic government to lead the nation to a market economy and a western slant—away from fundamentalist Moslem concerns.

2006

Peace is firmly entrenched in the Holy Land, and the biggest winner is Palestine, which gains huge financial dividends from Arab states' support.

2007

A devastating earthquake flattens large areas of Armenia, but instead of sending humanitarian help, neighboring Azerbaijan sends troops to attack Armenia in its time of woe.

2008

AIDS is out of control on the African continent. Draconian measures are forced upon Africans in hopes that someone can be saved. The UN enlists the reluctant government of the Camerouns to allow that country to be the quarantine site for all of Africa's AIDS patients.

2010

Nation after nation in Africa, decimated by internecine strife or disease, succumbs to government administration of the United Nations over vast territories. More than half the continent flies the blue and white UN flag over government centers.

The war against crime takes a positive turn when a young child becomes attracted to the idea of using cameras at intersections to keep an eye on criminals. The child develops amazing software that allows computers to lock on to suspects and to trail them to their lairs. Street crime becomes ancient history almost overnight. With evidence of the crime on videotape, its authenticity ensured by myriad backup sensors, the prosecutors have no trouble convicting anyone spotted by the crimestopping television cameras.

Armenians and Kurds, two groups with long histories of enmity toward each other, reach an underground agreement to unite in a battle against their common and historical foe, Turkey.

All new buildings in the United States will be constructed with virtual-reality firefighting systems built into the walls.

Embattled Uganda surprises the world by turning the corner against disease, political corruption, and military unrest to emerge as a dominant nation in Africa. It becomes a tourist mecca.

2011

After a long series of experiments in animals, the first use of a unique computer vaccine begins in human beings. The microscopic computers are injected into people with a family predisposition to cancer. The results are astounding. Not only will the devices work like a charm in every person—without regard to sex or body weight or body fat—but doctors will be able to pinpoint very early changes in cells that herald the onset of cancer, allowing earlier treatment and a much higher cure rate for even the most stubborn and deadly cancers.

Astronomers confirm that a chain reaction of minor moons around Jupiter have somehow bumped the larger moons of Jupiter, changed their orbits, and have sent the moons of Io and Ganymede onto a collision course.

2012

Pro-Cuban statehood is a major issue in the United States. Historians point out that if the United States had acted on a previous statehood movement for Cuba—one hundred years earlier in the early 1900s—a century of chaos for both Cuba and the United States would have been eliminated. Radical change in the government of the island leads to the nation becoming a US state.

Saudi Arabia proposes that it finance the protection of religious sites sacred to Islam throughout the world, including those in Israel. Agreement by the Israelis results in a de facto government of Palestine in Jerusalem and ends the stickiest questions of peace in the Holy Land.

2013

A horrible cyclone comes ashore in cyclone-prone Bangladesh. The destructive storm plows through mainly underpopulated territory, but fifty thousand people still lose their lives to the wind and water.

2014

A serious earthquake rumbles through the Adirondack mountains, leveling the village of Long Lake and causing months of tremors across upstate New York.

Nostalgic Americans begin migrating in droves to Casablanca, Morocco, opening dozens of taverns or coffee shops known as "Rick's" or "Cafe Americaine."

2015

Led by nationalist fervor, the Ukraine—the breadbasket of Europe—forges a series of new agreements that create a new power on the continent. The Ukraine, Belarus—also known as White Russia—and the Baltic states of Latvia, Lithuania, and Estonia agree to major economic and military pacts that at one stroke create a powerful armed force on the continent. The five states, led by virtual one-party leadership, unearth the oldest and foulest demagoguery to capture the jingoistic hearts of their countrymen. And they create a nuclear-powered military threat to all of Europe.

The Cincinnati Reds' club president and officers will be kidnapped by outraged fans who learn the club is planning to move the franchise. The officials are released after they agree to sell the club to locals who pledge to keep it in Cincinnati.

2016

Three years after the last cyclone, another storm churns through Bangladesh and neighboring India. The citizens of both countries breath a sigh of relief as just ten thousand people are killed.

2018

A massive earthquake in the Big Bear Lake area of Southern California cracks dams and sends millions of gallons of water down the Santa Ana wash, where it hurdles its banks and drowns an estimated hundred thousand people in San Bernardino and Riverside.

2019

The dreams, prosperity, and independence of Costa Rica is changed by a massive hurricane that crushes the east coast of the country. Urged by relatives of Americans living in Costa Rica, the US sends in massive aid and clerical and military assistance to help the nation recover. The troops and aides never leave and Costa Rica opts for statehood three years later.

The US government announces that its network of ocean sensors and spy satellites have given it complete surveillance of the entire ocean—above and below the surface. The system eliminates the need for remote ocean naval monitoring bases and it is abandoning many of them, including the base on Palmyra Atoll about one thousand miles southwest of Hawaii.

2020

The World Health Organization releases a secret report on AIDS in Africa, showing the numbing figures that more than forty million men, women, and children have died from the disease since 1980.

2021

Jupiter's moons of Io and Ganymede collide in the first live televised interplanetary cataclysm. Thousands of destructive asteroids are created by the impact—and those rocks are headed toward Earth.

2022

The Great War between China and India and Pakistan results in the deaths of more than twenty-eight million people. As the nations threaten to use nuclear weapons against each other, the United States ends the war by exploding its supersecret weapon—the awesome Thunderclap.

The Kaliningrad Crisis pits Russia against Poland and the Central Axis over a small territory of Russia on the Baltic Sea. When it appears that Kaliningrad is about to be overrun, Russia appeals for help from NATO and Germany sends troops, ships, and planes to its former territory to "protect" it. The interventions result in a stalemate for fifteen years.

Seventeen people die in the Sedona Incident when Native Americans on horseback raid and burn a development the Natives claim was built on sacred grounds in Arizona.

2023

On January 28, 2023, the second nuclear power plant disaster in two weeks will occur in Florida, causing the contamination of one hundred thousand acres of Florida coastline, directly and indirectly killing forty-eight thousand people over the next eight years, and creating a worldwide depression and chaos when nations shut down all nuclear power facilities due to massive protests.

2024

In Nogales, Mexico, across the border from Nogales, Arizona, a group of angry union members walk off the job in a wildcat strike. Gunfire erupts and quickly involves troops of both nations fighting each other.

Meanwhile, Americans and sympathetic Mexicans who are making good money from Americans and American tourists in San Jose de Cabo, at the tip of Baja California, and others in Tijuana, Mexicali, and Ensenada take over the local broadcast systems, declare the independence of Baja California from Mexico, and immediately request annexation by the United States.

Complications increase as tourist-conscious Yucatan declares that its citizens—mostly descendants of Mayan Indians—also want to be free of the corrupt and ineffectual government of Mexico City. The request for US military protection is approved by the US, which sends thousands of troops across the Yucatan Straits from Cuba.

2025

Kurdish terrorists explode an atomic bomb in downtown Ankara, the capital of Turkey, killing hundreds of thousands of people.

Just about every home in America is now wired and is online with the telecommunications superhighway—and industry and business pay for the hookups as well as reward homeowners for using the system.

2028

The first Hemlock Society "preparation" camp opens. The camps are named in honor of Dr. Jack Kevorkian, who had become an icon to the suicide-option minded. The first camp was opened in southern Sweden where there was little opposition.

2030

The stunning growth of the United States continues to the north, where Canada is coming apart. The industrious, wealthy, resource-rich, French-speaking province of Quebec demands so much favored-province status that the other provinces determine to abandon the commonwealth. First to jump ship are the maritime provinces of New Brunswick, Nova Scotia, Prince Edward Island, and Labrador. The four provinces on the eastern seaboard seek admission as one state—a request that is backed by the New England states and is approved quickly.

Then British Columbia and the Yukon Territory ask for admission as a single-state entity, which gives the United States an uninterrupted border from the Arctic Circle to the Yucatan Peninsula. The Canadian prairie provinces of Alberta, Saskatchewan, and Manitoba follow quickly behind the maritimes and the western provinces, eager to combine their cattle and grain-producing merchandise in the general US hopper.

By 2030 the success of the computer-vaccine system will remove any doubt about its ability to keep people healthy. Children will be required to have the vaccination just as certain as birth blood tests have been required for decades. Religious objections will continue to be allowed by the courts, but even most of the extreme religious groups will recognize the remarkable ability of the vaccination process to keep people alive and well and by 2050 universal vaccination will be virtually accomplished.

Oversaturation of the electronic highway by evangelical ministers cuts everyone's income and heralds the end of broadcast evangelism as a dominant power in the United States.

2031

Congress agrees to admit four different sections of Mexico as states: Baja California and a section of coastal Mexico on the opposite shore of the Gulf of California become state fifty-three; huge sections of Sonora, Chihuahua, Coahuila, and Nuevo León (Monterey) become state fifty-four; the Yucatan and the coast territory along the Caribbean that includes the important seaport of Veracruz is accepted as state fifty-five; and the territory along the Pacific shore, including Acapulco, is admitted a year later in 2032 as the fifty-sixth state. Independent Mexico is reduced to a small area along the Pacific, the intermountain desert which includes Durango, and Mexico City and its environs.

Major league baseball adds sixteen teams, making the sport truly international. Among the teams that will have a major impact on the game—the Holy Land Peacemakers.

2032

The Electric War will erupt in Alabama, where holdouts against the electronic superhighway will be defeated by the promoters of progress. No one will die in conflict between fundamentalists and progressives.

2033

When an attempt is made to vaccinate children, the first of the Red Cross Massacres occurs in the Central African Republic.

The Kevorkian Riot is the first and the last of the assaults on the Kevorkian camps in the United States. The unruliness of the mob, the televised documentation of the first shot being fired at the police, the attack against authority, and the horrendous assaults recorded against a few of the patients at the Kevorkian camp turn the nation against the anti-Kevorkians.

A home consultant—a member of one of the most secure professions on the twenty-first century—is successfully sued for failing to inform a home buyer he assisted that he was purchasing land that was a sacred burial ground of a midwestern tribe.

2034

Major league baseball sets in place a workable salary cap after rabid boosters among wealthy Arab and Jewish supporters of the Holy Land Peacemakers donate so much money to the Peacemakers that the club spends $74 million over their income on salaries for the top players in the world.

The man who was injected at birth with pig protein receives a xenograft—the heart of a pig. His body accepts the foreign tissue. He doesn't require rejection drugs, opening up a new field for the control of heart disease.

2037

Scientists try to derail a massive cyclone heading towards Bangladesh by exploding nuclear weapons in the Indian Ocean. A lot of fish die but the storm with winds approaching two hundred miles per hour never wavers from its course. It slams into the most populated areas of Bangladesh, killing an estimated two million people.

Russia agrees to allow a UN-sponsored plebiscite for its embattled territory of Kaliningrad. The voters decline independence or union with either Poland, Lithuania, Belarus, or Germany. Instead the territory opts to remain part of democratically-shaky Russia.

2040

On October 30, 2040, during one of the driest spells on record in Washington state, a quarter-mile-long meteor that was once part of one of the moons of Jupiter enters the atmosphere of earth. The friction between the meteor and the air causes the huge rock to superheat and melt and even burn. In fact almost a third of the rock, it is estimated, had disintegrated when, glowing brightly enough to turn darkened Seattle into day and roaring through the sonic barrier, the meteor sliced a two-hundred-mile crease across the Sierra Nevada mountains before cratering itself west of Spokane. It takes six months to put out all the forest fires caused by the streaking meteorite. The death toll is surprisingly small—officially put at 280 people (another one hundred people are killed fighting the fires or trying to escape fire-fighting equipment that raced to one blaze after another).

Virtually all the anti-Kevorkian legislation that had been on the books in several states is repealed. The camps now spread everywhere in the country, although areas around Boston and Chicago where there are strong religious commitments against suicide don't have camps for another decade.

The hottest franchise in America is the 211-Line, a delivery organization that promises to get your fax or computer on line within thirty minutes or your service charge is free.

2041

The Nobel Prize committee awards the prize in medicine posthumously to the man who had inoculated his son with pig protein, as thousands of babies are now being inoculated as regular practice to ward against future heart disease.

2042

The Roman Catholic Church elects the first American Pope, the first non-European in two thousand years to sit on the throne of St. Peter in the Vatican.

2043

A group of elite actors, athletes, writers, and industrialists announce that they are members of a religion based on the ancient Baal worship that held sway over the Middle East in 200 BC.

2044

The new city of Ankara is dedicated by Turkey which, while mourning the hundreds of thousands who died in the nuclear terrorist attack and decrying the forces that created the bomb, apologizes—more than a century after the fact—for the slaughter of tens of thousands of Armenians during World War I.

2045

Asteroid Cowboys manage to correctly place an atomic weapon on giant asteroid MEWS2-16, knocking the rock off its collision course with Earth, saving the planet.

All community and public buildings in the United States are retrofitted with virtual-reality firefighting equipment.

The Baalists persuade the United States government—for $4 billion—to lease the abandoned Palmyra Atoll as a place where the Baalists can pursue their religion in peace.

2048

The first colony to be designated as a permanent city gains its first inhabitants on the Moon. By the end of the century 150,000 people will be living in more than two dozen communities on the planet—with asteroid mining as the main source of income aside from tourism.

2050

One by one the nations of Africa have their independence restored. With a generation of universal education and progressive human rights–oriented governmental agencies in place through the auspices of the United Nations, the promise of America begins to be achieved. The deaths of millions of Africans through disease and strife actually helps position the nations for the future. They are self-sufficient in food production and are able to exploit their resources and join the world market.

2051

The long-dormant volcano Haleakala erupts on the Hawaiian island of Maui. Although the eruption is massive, few are lost because scientists had predicted the eruption far enough in advance to evacuate most citizens. The eruption heralds an era of new volcanic activity in the Pacific "Ring of Fire."

2052

A military coup overturns the government of Togo just six months after the UN forces leave, having declared that democracy has been successfully restored in the West African nation.

2054

A gigantic volcanic eruption thirty-four miles south-southeast of the big island of Hawaii sends massive tidal waves crashing into the island, devastating Hilo and other communities situated on the shores of the island. The tsunamis travel across the Pacific and cause damage as far away as northern California. While the death toll is minimal in most areas, damage runs into the billions of dollars in Hawaii and other Pacific islands. Especially hard hit is the Palmyra Atoll where the Baal worship commune is wiped out by forty-foot waves, which wash over the low-lying islets. But when the eruptions stop, the world discovers a new island has formed, and is later named Nene, after Hawaii's official bird.

2060

The San Diego Padres become victims of an anti-religious fervor in the country and change the name of the baseball team to the San Diego Gulls.

2061

The United States federal government reaches a landmark event: It completes the cleanup of the 250th Superfund hazardous waste site. There were originally 1,200 sites on the list. The government projects a complete cleanup of all those sites by 2150. No one believes it will be accomplished that soon.

2064

Fundamentalist Muslims attack the campus of the University of Cairo, slaughtering professors and students in a bloodbath captured live on campus television cameras that broadcast the horror worldwide on CNN. The brutal attack against the unarmed students and faculty creates a violent backlash that signals the demise of the Muslims as a political force around the world.

2065

Firemen become obsolete. Just about every structure now has virtual-reality equipment to fight fires. There is no longer reason for firemen to zoom around cities in trucks.

2068

The IBM-Exxon space expedition lifts off from Spacebase Borneo. On board is a crew of twenty—ten men and ten women who are matched for compatibility, intellect, and sexuality. The crew includes space pilots, navigators, doctors, engineers, and scientists.

2070

The first colony on Mars is declared a permanent settlement by the United Nations after the population of Mars City exceeds five thousand people.

2074

A scandal among the most vituperative of the antireligionists brands the antireligion movement as a corrupt religion itself. Organized religions experience a slow recovery, despite occasional setbacks.

2075

By the third quarter of the twenty-first century there are sixty-five United States of America, and the red, white, and blue flag covers every territory in the Caribbean and in North and Central America except for a few tiny islands, Quebec, and the slice of Mexico and Guatemala that successfully bucked the tide of American nationalism and expansionism.

2077

The new Mars permanent settlement of Ares City declares itself a Religious-Free Zone, prohibiting the practice of any form of religion—an offshoot of the antireligious sentiment that had been building since the late 2050s and 2060s. However, the prohibition becomes unworkable and after one month the city repeals the prohibition and declares itself a Religious Strife-Free Zone and constructs a unique chapel to be used by all religions.

2082

After forty years of relatively smooth sailing and controversy-free activity despite antireligion thunder under a series of progressive North American popes, the Roman Catholic Church elects another American—but this is the first pope who is an African American. His election rekindles smoldering problems of race within the church and several parishes break away from devotion to Rome.

2084

The reign of the first black pope of the Roman Catholic Church is cut short when he develops cancer. His grace under pressure and in the face of death gains the admiration of the world. His death is followed by the election of the first Pope to have been born in the Holy Land.

2085

Archeologists in the late twenty-first century, around 2085, astound the world by claiming the rediscovery of the city of Stanleyville—a major city in Zaire lost to the junglization of Africa for generations.

2086

Another reorganization and expansion of major league baseball occurs in 2086, creating the World Series Tournament.

On what would have been considered mid-summer of 2086 on Earth, the IBM-Exxon Explorer deep spacecraft sends an unmanned mini-probe to enter the atmosphere of the fourth planet of Alpha Centauri. Human explorers follow and so does the discovery of a race of intelligent humanoids.

2090

The first reports of the remarkable eighteen-year-old IBM-Exxon Journey to the Stars Expedition are received on Earth. The reports tell of amazing life on one planet surrounding the star, Alpha Centauri, the nearest neighbor to our solar system.

The Explorer spacecraft actually reaches the Alpha Centauri system in 2086, but no one on Earth knows about it for four years, so 2090 is recorded as the date on which humans reach another solar system. Purists try for years to get the world to agree that 2086 was really the proper date, but no one listens to that. People just remember where they are on the date that we find out we are not alone in the universe.

2097

In 2097 there are eighty-four teams in major league baseball, and the game is played on every continent, although professional baseball hasn't taken a toehold in Antarctica as yet. In addition to the major league levels there are literally thousands of minor leagues around the world.

2098

The first settlement on the volcanic island of Nene is established. The small community of scientists—geologists and volcanists, mainly—set up houses on the northern tip of the island, far from the sulfuric fumeroles that smoke constantly on the southern end of the island, which continues to add land mass just about every day.

FASCINATING BOOKS
OF SPIRITUALITY
AND PSYCHIC DIVINATION

CLOUD NINE: A DREAMER'S DICTIONARY
by Sandra A. Thomson
77384-8/$6.99 US/7.99 Can

SECRETS OF SHAMANISM:
TAPPING THE SPIRIT POWER
WITHIN YOU
by Jose Stevens, Ph.D. and Lena S. Stevens
75607-2/$5.99 US/$6.99 Can

TAROT IN TEN MINUTES
by R.T. Kaser
76689-2/$10.00 US/$12.00 Can

THE LOVERS' TAROT
by Robert Mueller, Ph.D., and Signe E. Echols, M.S.,
with Sandra A. Thomson
76886-0/$11.00 US/$13.00 Can

SEXUAL ASTROLOGY
by Marlene Masini Rathgeb
76888-7/$10.00 US/$12.00 Can